Afrikan Spirituality for Children of the Afrikan Diaspora

By Blak Pantha

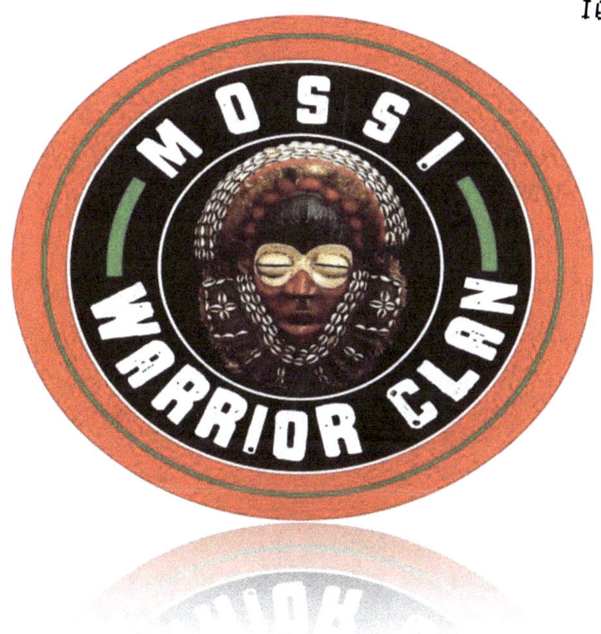

Kofi Piesie/Mossi Warrior Clan

Printed in the United States of America

ISBN 979-8-9896372-9-4

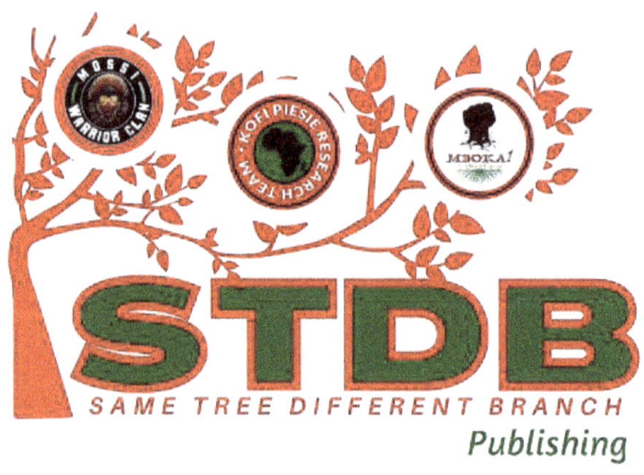

Table of Contents

Afrikan Spirituality for the Children of the Afrikan Diaspora

Introduction

I am a man of many names, but you can call me Brother Ben, Blak Pantha or Ògúnjìnmí. I am a pan Afrikan, lecturer, author, proud member of many organizations, Ògún priest and Co-founder of the Mossi Warrior Clan scholarship group. I am an advocate of African Spirituality and use the principles of these ancient practices to solve problems within the black community and in the diaspora worldwide. Having traveled to KMT, South Afrika, Senegal and Gambia I am an avid researcher and scholar that focuses on sound methodology, primary and well verified secondary sources as his means of providing information to Afrikan people.

I decided to write this book because I see a need for this information not only in the conscious or woke community but the black community as a whole. We are children of the diaspora and as those Black Afrikan people we are largely drawn to spiritual practices of all regions of the earth. Whether this be Hinduism, Buddhism, or New Age spiritual practices we seem to have an affinity for practices of the metaphysical. What's interesting about this phenomenon is we rarely look to Afrika for these practices, or we try to trick our minds into believing that all practices come from Afrika because life came from Afrika, so it doesn't matter.

For now, I will say that is simply historically, socially, politically, and spiritually inaccurate and later in this book I will get into why. Information is needed to be dispersed about our spiritual systems from our ancestors and current people in the continent of Afrika. It is my opinion that we can glean great knowledge from these systems and use these ancient practices to improve our condition globally.

This is my contribution to fill the gap in knowledge we have about our ancient Afrikan systems. We will talk about what is Afrikan spirituality and go over various systems. We will talk about why Afrikan spirituality is important to Afrikan liberation. We will introduce a new term that will serve as an umbrella to the Afrikan Spirituality moniker. We will talk about how we already engage in some of these practices and don't know it but first we must dispel some rumors and give some propensities of the community that harms the research of Afrikan spirituality. After that I will take you on a journey that involves instructing you on what it means to be a child of the Afrikan diaspora, what ki.môyo is and why it's important. We will go over the fundamentals of spiritual practices you have heard of and some you have not heard of. We will introduce you to the concept of the community of memory and give my final thoughts, references, and book recommendations. I truly hope this text is fulfilling and you learn vital information that transforms your thinking.

What is the Woke/Conscious Community

Let's start with the primary community that has engaged in spiritual information and teaching for the black experience in America. This community is key in the diaspora and has a lot of influence so it's imperative that we discuss it. I'm talking about the conscious/woke community. First let me say I was a part of this community from 2010 - 2022. I have seen its successes and its failures. I've seen the brilliant minds that have emerged from this community, and I've seen its lesser minds promote falsehoods purposely in the attempts to collect a check and followers. To accurately talk about Afrikan spirituality within this community we must define what it is. Only then can we discuss its pitfalls and how Afrikan spirituality can help. So, what is the woke/conscious community? Understand this is a working definition I have created through my decade of dealing in this dynamic. There is no official definition for this phenomenon. I define the woke/conscious community as a collective of minds dedicated to the betterment of Afrikan people, breaking away from false narratives taught in history and empowering each other with information that was never taught in primary education. That sounds like a great definition, right? Well, we also have to talk about the sum of spiritual propensities of the members of this community both positive and negative.

Spiritual propensities of the conscious/Woke community.

Half Hindus or what I like to call Third eye blind.

Making things up and attributing everything to ancient KMT(Egypt)

Dedication to offshoots of Afrikan systems

Half Hindus or Third Eye Blind

Black people in this community tend to attempt to instruct you about Chakras, Kundalini and the Third eye. You would think from what I just said we would be discussing Hinduism but sadly we aren't. People try to attach these phenomena to ancient KMT. If not, they will tell you that the Indians didn't create this system and that some Afrikans migrated there and taught them this. Lastly, they will tell you that these Indians are Afrikan themselves, so Hinduism is Afrikan culture. A simple google search will inform you that none of these practices come from Afrika and were Asian inventions. You wouldn't find the third eye in KMT no matter where you look in KMT (Both Ra and Heru have two eyes you know) and simple genetics will show people from India and people from Afrika are not the same. Kundalini is also a product of Hinduism but since its categorized as a serpent Afrikans in America have attached it to practices that has nothing to do with Kundalini. Benin is probably the best example of the veneration of snakes in Afrika. They have a temple of pythons where it is illegal to kill a snake. This is because they are believed to represent ancestors. Does that sound like a power going up your spine like kundalini? It probably doesn't because these are two different concepts from two different cultures. Along with the kundalini are chakras and in the interest of attaching them to Afrika you have those that attach the new age colors of chakras to the Orisa Osumare because he is represented by a rainbow or rainbow serpent. When one studies Hinduism closely you will find that I used the word new age colors for a reason. The colors you see currently representing chakras are called Newtonian colors and you won't find them representing chakras in any spiritual system. To make matters worse all the components of Hinduism that we have discussed are created by people that have one of if not the worst caste system on earth. This system puts darker Indians at the bottom and call them the untouchables. You must ask yourself why are we involved in a cultural appropriation cycle with people that don't value people that have dark skin?

Making Things Up about KMT

KMT or ancient Egypt seems to be the first stopping point for the conscious community member when they leave the church, mosque, or synagogue. Sadly, when one transitions from God, Allah or Yahweh to RA, Ptah and Asar they frequently take the ideas, principles, and beliefs from the Abrahamic faiths and superimpose them of the Egyptian deities. Ra becomes God, Heru becomes Jesus, Aset become Mary etc. Very few people take the time to learn to read the Mdw Ntchr (hieroglyphs) so they can read and interpret Egyptian thought. Instead, we make up stories about the Egyptians creating our own folk etymology and selling ourselves short instead of learning about these great Afrikan people. We say things like the Ancient Egyptians created the light bulb, they had helicopters and created the Zodiac symbols. For two of these claims, we must go to the temple of Dendara in Ancient Egypt (See picture below). Unfortunately, these depictions are not light bulbs in mdw ntr the name of these glyphs are called < iturty >. They are used as determinatives or in variated forms in the pyramid text of unis., [Les Inscriptions des Pyramides de Saqqarah 1894] and other inscriptions in the Temple of Dendera. From the mdw nTr website we find an accurate article giving clarity of what these glyphs convey and accurate translation s from the Dendera Temple by Baba/Sba Wudjau Iry Maat:

The appearance of a "bubble" surrounding the serpent represents the protective enclosure of the sky, the environment in which the sun is born. It is associated with the womb or placenta of Nut who swallows the sun each night and gives birth to the sun each morning. There are numerous scenes depicting Nut with feet and arms bent over as the sun is near her mouth and near her womb. The "bubble" surrounding the serpent also represents an actual hieroglyph used in the ancient Egyptian language. The mdw-nTr (hieroglyphic) word itrty /itr.ty/ iterty "primordial sanctuaries, sacred place, sacred palace" is attested in abundance at Edfu, Karnak, and Dendera.[1]

---

[1] Ntr Nb Pr Ntr Research Center of African History and Ancient Studies and Wudjau Iry Maat

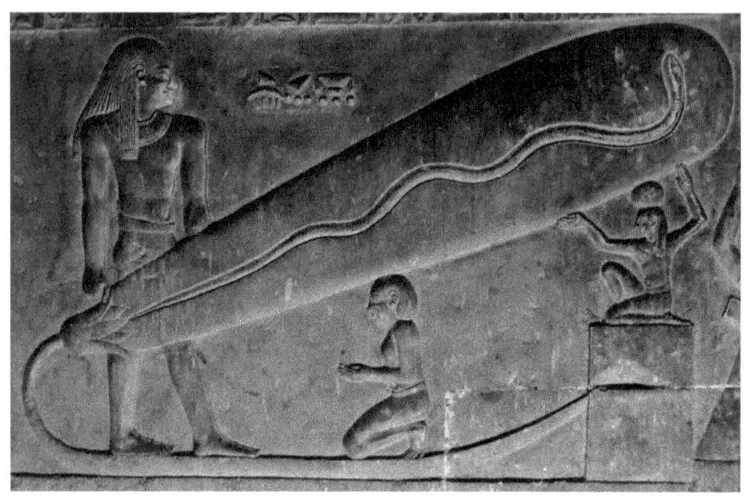

Zodiacs are indeed in the temple of Dendara as well (please see below), but the Ancient Egyptians did not create them. The temple of Dendara is the only temple in which zodiac astrology signs exist but this project was commissions under Greek rule and does not appear in any other time period than under Greek rule. Ultimately Astrology is of Babylonian and Greek origin and not Afrikan. You probably don't believe me so let's do this what does the word Zodiac mean and what language is it? Answer the word Zodiac means cycle or circle of little animals in Greek. Ok you probably still don't believe me well the chapel where we find these zodiac signs began construction during the Ptolemaic period. For those that aren't familiar the Ptolemy period is when Greeks ruled KMT. Sylvie Cauville of the Centre for Computer-aided Egyptological Research at Utrecht

University and Éric Aubourg dated it to 50 BCE through an examination of the configuration it shows of the five planets known to the Egyptians, a configuration that occurs once every thousand years, and the identification of two eclipses[2]. If this is to be believed, then the Ancient Egyptians were long gone being that the last Afrikan ruler of KMT was Nectanbo II finishing his rule around 340 BCE.

---

[2] Marchant, Jo (5 July 2010). "Decoding the ancient Egyptians' stone sky map". *New Scientist*.

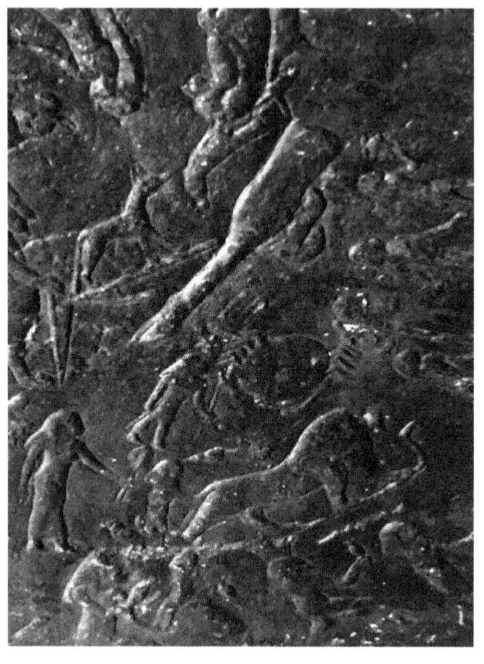

For the last claim we go to the holy city for the Ancient Egyptians which is Abydos or Abtu. Is this tomb you will find a relief that people say looks like helicopters, tanks, and other inventions the ancient Egyptians didn't have. What are these glyphs that look like modern inventions you ask? The glyphs are a result of both erosion of the stone surface (evident elsewhere in the temple) and the process of filling in and re-carving the stone to replace some of the original hieroglyphics. The technical term for such a surface that has been written on more than once is called a palimpsest. The usurping and modifying of inscriptions were common in ancient Egypt throughout its history.

The glyph here were modified at least once in antiquity, and perhaps twice. Some of the filling has fallen out in places where the older and the newer inscriptions overlap, and the result is unique and odd-looking.

The text is part of the titulary ("title") of Ramesses II which replaced the royal titulary of Seti I (Men Maat Ra Seti) that was originally carved into the stone. From the latter half of the 5th dynasty on, the royal titulary consisted of five title or /rn wr/ "great names." These names expressed the power, might, and overall mission statement of the King. Often times, these 5 titles were grouped as a long Royal Titulary in temples. There was an apparent change in the scale of the glyphs which also makes it difficult to discern (Please see image below).

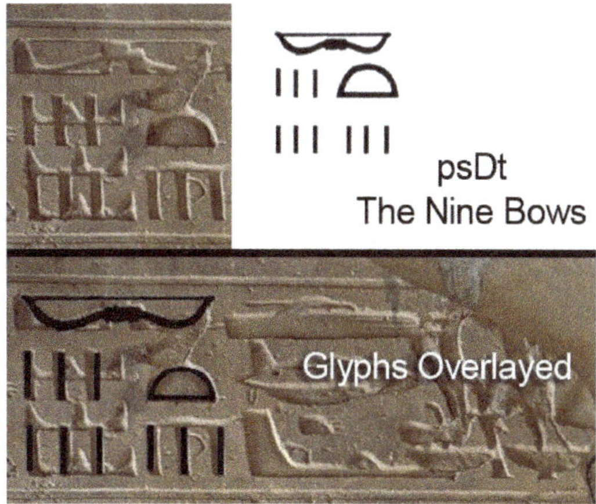

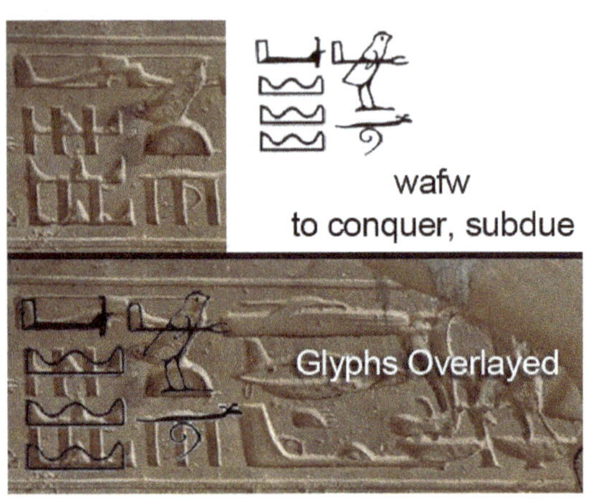
wafw
to conquer, subdue
Glyphs Overlayed

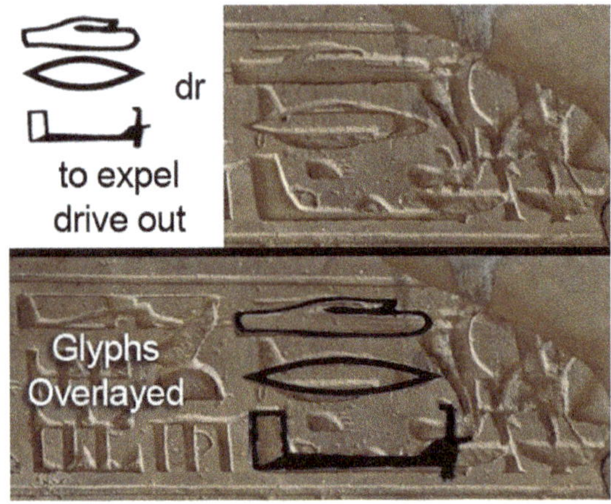
dr
to expel
drive out
Glyphs
Overlayed

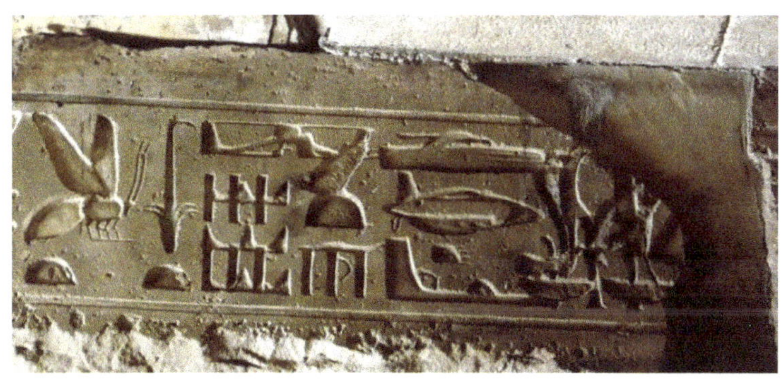

Dedication to Offshoots of Afrikan systems

There are many offshoots of Afrikan spiritual systems because of the trans-Atlantic slave trade. These systems went to countries outside of Afrika and developed their own cultural influences. From what I observed there are many people (dare I say the majority) that are content with Afrikan root but Spanish in practice. This typically happens amongst Òrìṣà and Palo practitioners. Since these practices have Afrikan roots most people don't seem to know or mind the western religious and Spanish influences they denote. When one tries to shift the practice back to the root of the continent that everyone claims they love they are met with attitude and hostility. Strange behavior from people that identify as Afrikan. All though the Afrikan roots are ever present there are many differences oof the root and the branch. Language, rituals, and cultural perspective often get lost in translation and migration. The end result is something very different from its original form. That's not to say what's right and wrong but rather what is traditional and what is now its own way. An example of this can be seen amongst the Yoruba and the Lucumi people in Cuba. The Lucumi people practice Regla de Ocha which is derived from Ìṣẹ̀ṣe amongst the Yoruba people of Southwestern Nigeria. In Regla de Ocha they place a deity called Ògún in an Iron caldron. Being that Ògún is the deity of iron you would thing you would see this is Ìṣẹ̀ṣe but you will not see this because it's taboo to place Ògún in an enclosed container in Ìṣẹ̀ṣe. So, you see how important it is to decide which way one wants to practice. If it's traditional west Afrikan systems i.e. the root, then you will practice a particular way that will be visibility different from the branch and offshoot.

What it Means to be a Child of the Afrikan Diaspora

We are a people connected by a great tragedy and we share DNA with people that fought, died, ran, and endured for us to be alive today. No matter where you are outside of the mother continent, and you are sub-Saharan or black you are connected to this phenomenon, and these are the historical facts that bind us together. There are so many facets of being a child of the diaspora that we can explore. Let's look at it from a genetic standpoint. According to research conducted by Linda Heywood and John Thornton advancements in DNA research have shed light on the multifaceted makeup and origins of today's African Americans. In fact, most of today's African American population can trace their ancestry back to one of just 46 ethnic groups. Three large regions of Atlantic Africa were the major contributors to the slave trade: Upper Guinea, including the modern countries of Senegal, Mali, Gambia, Guinea, Sierra Leone and Liberia; Lower Guinea, including the southern portions of eastern Ivory Coast, Ghana, Togo, Benin and Nigeria; and West Central Africa, which encompassed mostly the western portions of the Democratic Republic of Congo and Angola.[3] Look at all the Afrikan countries associated with

[3] LINDA HEYWOOD AND JOHN THORNTON PHD

this genetic research now think about the tribes associated with all of these nation sates. There is honeycomb like pockets of ethnic groups that exist in all of these nation states. All of that history, experiences, knowledge, and culture destabilized by the horrid great tragedy known as the transatlantic slave trade. All of this genetic material has millions of possibilities of gene expression within Afrikan Americans. According to an article by Steven J. Micheleti entitled Genetic Consequences of the Transatlantic Slave Trade in the Americas previous genetic studies focusing on people of African descent across the Americas found that most African Americans in the United States have more African ancestry from populations that lived near present-day Nigeria than from populations that lived elsewhere in Atlantic Africa.[4] The tribes of these Nigerians that we share DNA with have been traced to be Yorùbá, Hausa, Igbo, Ijaw, Efik, Igala, Kalabari, Itsekiri, Ibibio, and Edo. These genetic studies further the discussion and point to the fact that not only are we Afrikan people by majority on average but we are also still connected to the source of our existence by ethnic groups that still exist in Afrika today. Imagine being able to connect with people

---

[4] Genetic Consequences of the Transatlantic Slave Trade in the Americas by Steven J. Micheleti

that are your family from an entire time period before you existed. It's possible due to our unique experience.

Let's look at what it means to be a child of the diaspora spiritually. Afrikan people in Amerika come from a spiritual heritage that most of us have not taken the time to tap into. We have a spiritual history that most of us are in gross ignorance of. If the average Afrikan American was honest with themselves, they would admit that when it comes to Afrikan spiritual traditions (falsely labeled religions) they don't have a clue and those that have an inkling of one only know random facts about Egypt. Egypt is a great study but notice how earlier in this chapter their DNA was not mentioned amongst the several countries we have a direct connection to. It stands to reason that a people that were ripped from their homes due to the slave trade will try to do everything in their power to recover their history. We have done just that for generations, but we forgot about our spiritual history. We as a whole did not go after our traditions that come from the continent with the same vigor as we went after our general history. This is largely because of the great impact foreign religions have had such as Christianity and Islam. We accepted the religions of two slave trades, and they became a permanent part of our experience.

During the Arab slave trade was when west Afrika came in contact with Allah and for 1300 years it was beat into us. After was the Trans-Atlantic Slave trade where Jesus was shoved down our throats for roughly 300 more years. These actions severed our connection to the power we have an inheritance to. The spiritual power that exists in many Afrikan tribes to this day. Afrikan child of the diaspora it is time we all reconnect to the source that permeates through us all. We have tried Allah's way and we have tried Jesus way and we are still at the bottom of society scrapping for crumbs. It's time we tried our ancestor's way. Later in this book we will specifically go over many systems that we can connect to and many more that are waiting for us to return to them. Afrikan child of the diaspora its time.

What is Afrikan Spirituality?

Afrikan spirituality is an identifier of the amalgamation of the several spiritual practices that come out of the continent. Essentially, it's the indigenous systems of Afrikans across the continent whose goal is to manifest energies, worship natural forces in the universe and venerate progenitors and ancestors. These energies we manifest are personified as deities or as some say Gods. One should note that the concept of God or Gods is vastly different in Afrika than it is in other countries around the world. To get a better understanding of what we as Afrikan spiritual traditionalist mean when we use the term Afrikan spirituality I would like to introduce a term from our Kikongo brothers and introduced to me by my brother Asar Imhotep. This term is Ki.môyo, it means literally heart referring to the essential and vital part of the person but culturally it represents force energy or dynamism and life through vitality and power. Dr K. Kia Bunseki Fu-Kiau from the Kongo (Congo Presently) in his text Digging up the past gives a detailed account of what Ki.môyo is. He states "The Bântu religion is not animism or animalism; neither are the Bântu animists nor animalists. The Bântu people are "vitalists", this is accepting themselves as weIl as everything in the universe as part of "N'kîngu a môyo", the principle of life in its wholeness. Their religion deals principally with Force and Vitality. A religion that does not believe in any physical being, but in "Ngolo ye môyo mu dingo-dingo" - Force and life through dingo-dingo, the natural way of life and change. This religion can be called "dynamo·-vitalism," or Kimôyo."[5] No matter if it is a traditional Afrikan system from the east, west, north or south this definition most likely fits the narrative of Ki.môyo in some for or fashion. Long ago in classical ancient Afrika there was what Dr. Kyosa Kajungu called the Afrikan super information highway. This was when priest, and other learned men of different Afrikan traditions would travel and share ideas, customs, ritual and language with other learned men of different Afrikan spiritual traditions. Credo Mutwa makes mention of this phenomena in his book Zulu Shaman: Dreams, Prophecies, and Mysteries (Song of the Stars), partly because of this information highway lots of Afrikan traditions have a similar feel and order about them and it is because of this fact that we feel comfortable using this term ki.môyo.

---

[5] K. Kia Bunseki Fu-Kiau Digging Up the Past

Why is AfrIkan spirituality so important to the AfrIkan?

Ki.môyo is the essence of Afrikan people globally, it's a part of our culture and gives us our lens which we look through to interpret reality. Culture is the arts and other manifestations of human intellectual achievement regarded collectively.[6] Culture is our fence, and it keeps out foreign influences that are to our detriment as Afrikan people. Culture gives us the ability to process information. Culture cannot exist outside of ourselves, it is in our minds but expressed through ki.môyo, arts, songs, poetry, proverbs, language and more. Identity and personality are cultural instruments, this is a part of how culture defends itself. When you distort a person's culture you distort their ability to process information and this is the first step in enslaving a people, you make them assimilates to your culture and therefore erase theirs. When African theologians took over the colonial missions, they had to invent ways of integrating these missions into the cultural ecology of African communities of memory. They have written endlessly to repudiate all the derogatory concepts that were coined by colonial scholars. A partial list of these concepts includes paganism,

[6] The Oxford English Dictionary definition of Culture

idolatry, ancestor worship, animism, juju, mana, voodoo, witchcraft, and polytheism. African theologians opposed such concepts and are still fighting the ghosts of this language of derision.[7] Culture is a historical product so therefore so is ki.môyo. Through time we become what Dr. Kykosa Kajangu calls a community of memory.[8] We have created a shred living memory in which is passed down from generation to generation. Let this circle be Unbroken![9] It is imperative to our survival that we glean the lessons from our golden age as a people and implement them into our current reality for the purpose of solving problems. This is how we win, and this is how we fight! We must keep our traditions alive through celebrating and practicing them today. Ki.môyo is also important because of a few concepts. Those are liberation through education and character development above all else. Allow me to explain the first time I heard the term liberation through education I was in Fort Worth Texas at an event which is called RBG weekend. This is an annual event in which the colors of the pan African flag are celebrated. It is a weekend of music, market

---

[7] Beyond the Colonial Gaze: Reconstructing African Wisdom Traditions By Dr. Kykosa Kajangu

[8] Beyond the Colonial Gaze: Reconstructing African Wisdom Traditions By Dr. Kykosa Kajangu

[9] Let the Circle Be UnBroken By Marimba Ani

and education. One of the leaders of this movement Baba Amin was the one that introduced me to this concept. He runs an Afrikan centered school in that area and transforms young men and women lives through Afrikan centered education. You will often here the phrase unlock the chain around your brain, well Afrikan centered education does just that. You will also hear the phrase the children are our future and I ask what kind of future is there for an Afrikan child that assimilates into western imperialism and systemic racism? Our community of memory will be burned to the ground and replaced with other memories, the same type of memories that enslaved us. There is an anti-intellectual movement within the conscious community/woke community that attempts to derail the liberation through education model. These are some of the worst of us and they are spiritually, intellectually lazy. We must identify them and cast them out or continue to be taken advantage of by their theatrics and scamming establishments. Character above all else is a concept I have been pushing in the community due to its importance in multiple ki.môyo systems across the continent. Let me give a few examples Ome: This is the highest moral category among the Igbo and contains values and norms which aim at upholding, preserving, fostering, and enhancing the life of the community. This community is peopled by the living and the dead. The concrete manifestation of Ome is Omenala.[10] Orunmila also taught that humans must move beyond moralities of convenience to a morality of sacrifice, i.e., self-giving in a real, meaningful, and sustained way. The Odu Ogbe'Fun says that "one who makes a small sacrifice will have a small result." Morality is the prime consideration for African oratory and public discourse. The power of Nommo appears to be in proportion to the moral character of a speaker, not just the person's oratorical skill.[11] The number one important thing ki.môyo does for us in the diaspora is character development and most of us need it BADLY! The number two important thing ki.môyo does for us is teaching us respect for the earth and nature. The number three most important thing ki.môyo does for us is the honoring of our lineage. We can have all the money, all the technology, all the great ideas we want but with bad character, disrespect of our earth, and no sense of AfrIkan pride we will lose our way again! There is no way around character improvement and its need for advancement. IWA Rere is described as good character in the Yorùbá Language. It refers to the moral quest of all Yorùbá

---

[10] The Igbo Paradigm Chika J. B. Gabriel Okpalike Nnamdi Azikiwe University 2015:8
[11] Character the most important ingredient in AfrIkan Spirituality By Blak Pantha

people and all practitioners of Yorùbá culture and traditions. It is the foundation of interaction and the basis of building and blessing within time. We speak about nation building all the time, but we must fix our character to do that. "With character comes strength honor, responsibility, and all the things are conducive to nation building.[12]" – Asar Imhotep. "It is only the Characterless that goes down permanently.[13]" Improving our character is how we circle the wagons and strengthen the conscious/woke community. Without that effort to constantly improve our character through the tradition of ki.môyo we will continue this cycle of violence and ignorance and as the elders say we will continue to be deaf, dumb and blind!

---

[12] Personal Quote from Asar Imhotep

[13] Personal Quote from Marcus Garvey in his speech called Real Character

Returning To a Practice We Already Engage In

Afrikans in the diaspora must realize that we engage in Afrikan cultural practices every day without realizing it. I spoke earlier about the community of memory and what that means for us culturally. Well, what if I told you that even now 500 years later, we have unconsciously preserved Afrikan practices in the diaspora? You probably are aware but at the same don't know to what extent. In this chapter I will give serval examples of how we engage in Afrikan cultural and mostly spiritual practices all the time.

Dice and Dominos

Dice and dominos have become a stable at black family gathering, and street corners. These games have become culturally apart of the black experience in America, but few know why we are drawn to these games. For the answer we must look at former president of the united stated slave quarters. Found there was a hand-carved bone domino is a "double three" tile with drilled indentations and no accompanying paint or enamel. Given the quality of the tile, it is likely that it was part of a mass-produced set. Similar examples have been found in a slave quarter dwelling at Thomas Jefferson's Monticello, Virginia and in a British soldiers' barracks at Signal Hill, Newfoundland. Beginning in the mid-nineteenth century, many domino tiles were comprised of a thin bone strip tacked to an ebony backing, suggesting that this example may have been made prior to this period[14]. Now why would Afrikan slaves be seemingly playing a game of dice and dominoes (see attached picture)? Well, who told you that these tools were only used for games? When we example bone divination in some cultures, the bones, shells, and/or nuts that are to be thrown are left in their natural state; in

[14] Digital Archaeological Archive of Comparative Slavery https://www.daacs.org/galleries/triplex/

other cultures, they may be shaped and marked, much like dice, dominoes, or the cut cowrie shells used in Erindilogun divination amongst the Yorùbá people.[15] Throwing the bones to access the advice of ancestors is an alternative practice to the exhausting ritual of possession by the ancestor. In a typical session, a patient will visit the Sangoma and the Sangoma must determine what the affliction is or the reason the patient has come to them for help. The patient or diviner throws bones on the floor, which may include animal vertebrae, dominoes, dice, coins, shells, and stones, each with a specific significance to human life.[16] It is most probable that these slaves were not just playing games but even if they were they were attracted to this game because they saw something familiar to them from their ancient practices and therefore accessing that community memory.

---

15 http://readersandrootworkers.org/wiki/Category:Throwing_the_Bones_and_Reading_Other_Natural_Curios

16 Africa in my bones. Claremont: New Africa Books Cumes, David (2004).

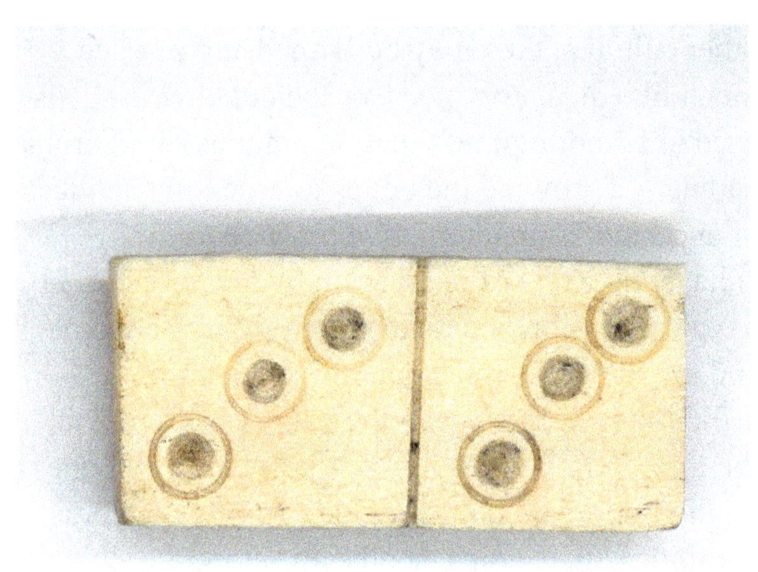

Afrikan Hair Styles We Rock

When you read the title of this part of this chapter you probably thought I was going to show a bunch of female hairstyles huh? Well, I'm going to show you those later but let's start with the fellas. Let's look at this traditional Mask found in Nigeria. I always say if you want to see how the people of an area looked you must look at their art and how they depict themselves. A mask of the Ogoni, who live in the hinterland of the Niger delta in southeastern Nigeria. The mask displays the characteristic features of the Ogoni style: it is carved from light-colored wood and relatively small. Its face, with the small, wide, upwards curved nose, is colored in white. Above, it wears a high, rounded and black-dyed 'towering hairstyle' (or cap?). Also, its ears, the round scarification marks on both temples, the outlines of its slit eyes and the wide mouth are black. Typical for the masks of the Ogoni are the common, large, hinged jaws, which allow an Ogoni mask to 'speak'. With 15 'teeth' made of wooden pegs, which were inserted in the lower jaw. The movable lower jaw is attached to the mask head at left and right by means of fiber cords. A 'classical' Ogoni mask, with old, partially shiny usage patina on the front and in particular on the rear edge. A small, old fracture on the forehead.[17] Let's draw a comparison to modern day styles. (See Picture Below)

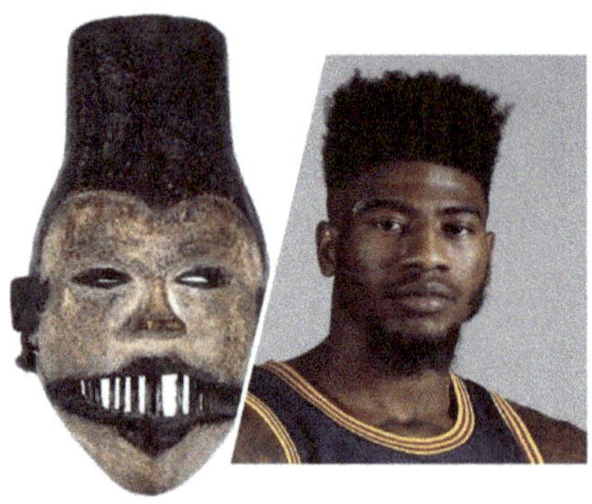

Let's look at another comparison picture from the same people of the same area.

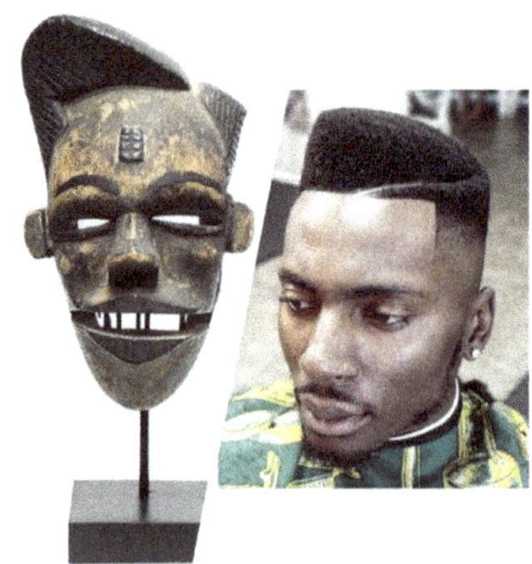

[17] Africa in my bones. Claremont: New Africa Books Cumes, David (2004).

Like I said earlier we are already engaging in Afrikan practices, but we just don't understand the power behind what we are doing. We know our brother love their waves as well, but do we understand that waves were not something we just up and created in America and the diaspora? Let's look at some examples.

Brothers in Ghana

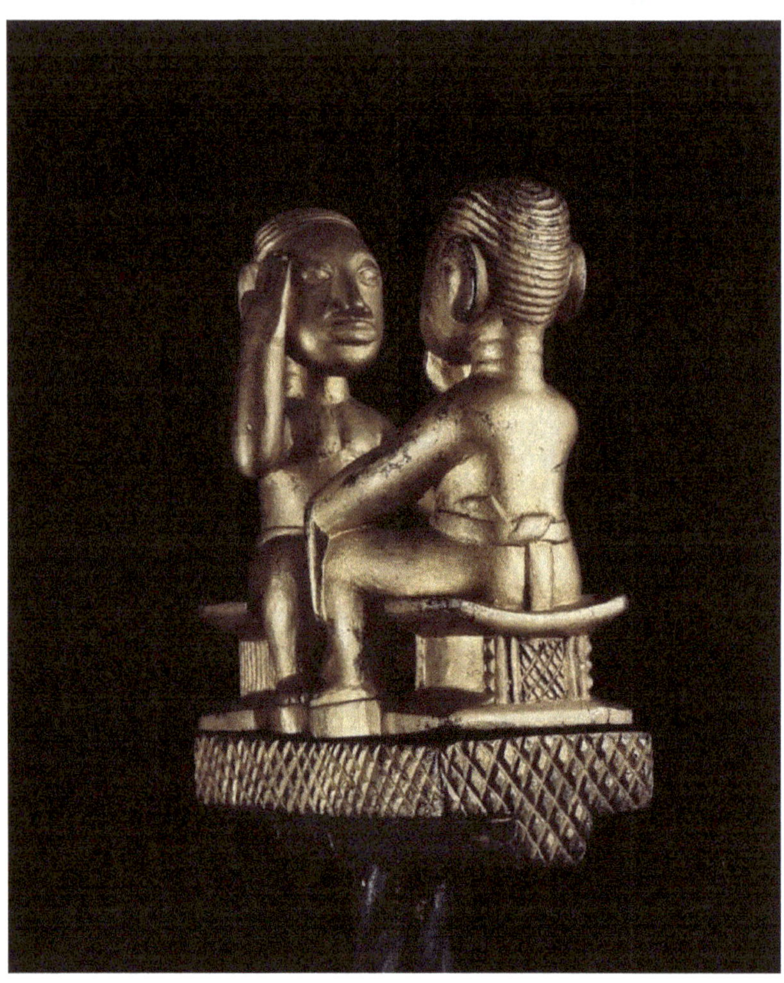

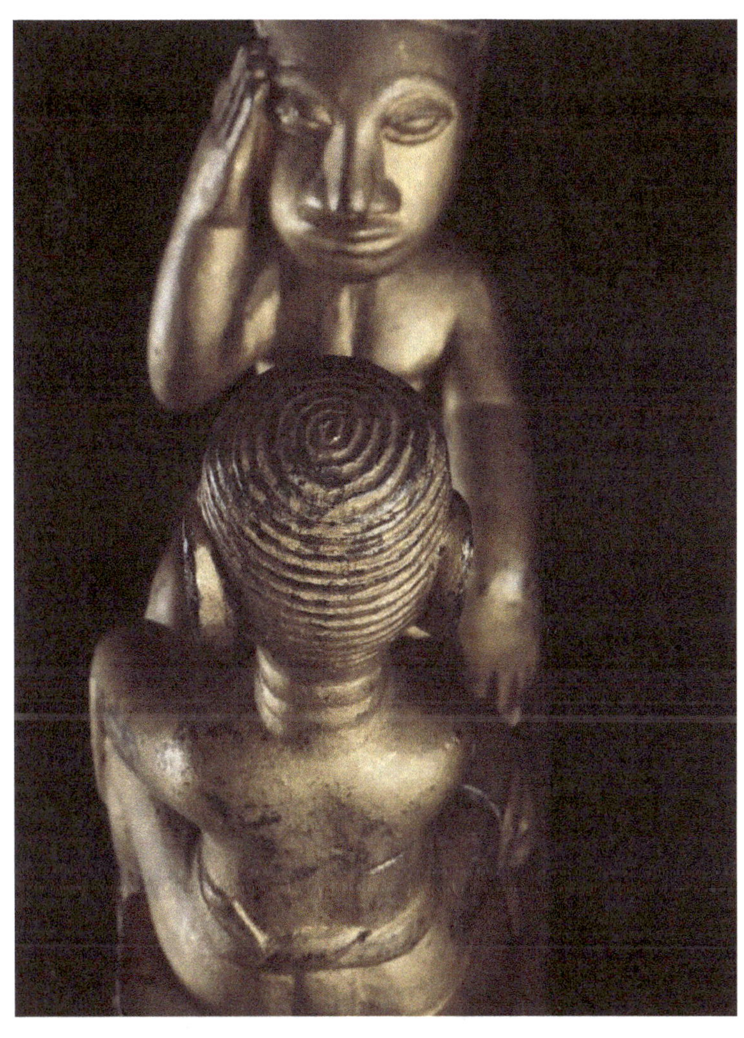

A Brother in Benin City (Present day Edo Kingdom in Nigeria)

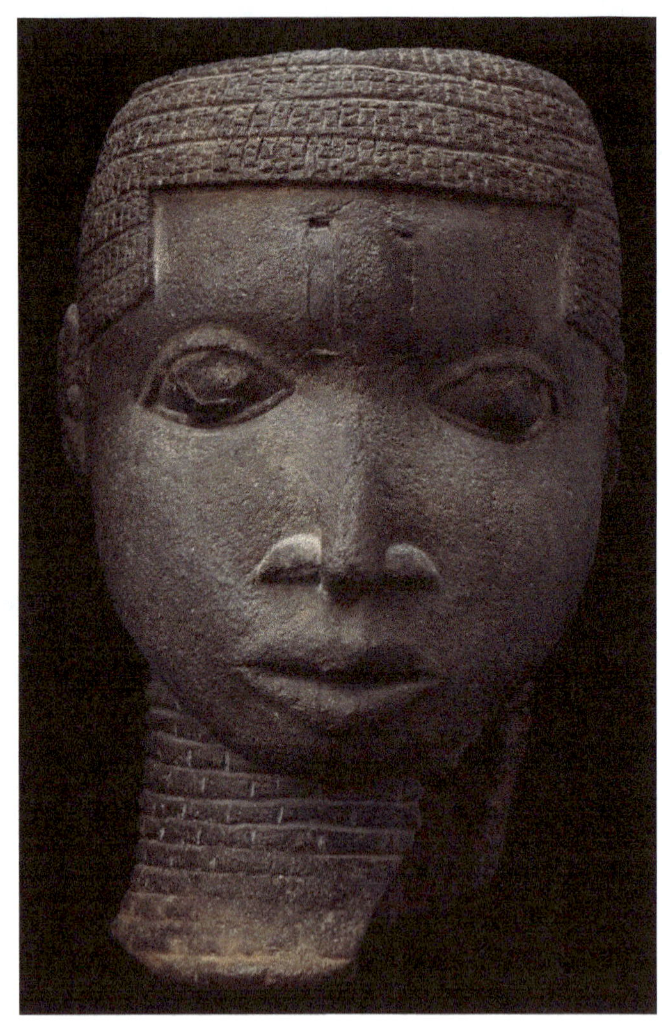

Bro Mekaure from KMT

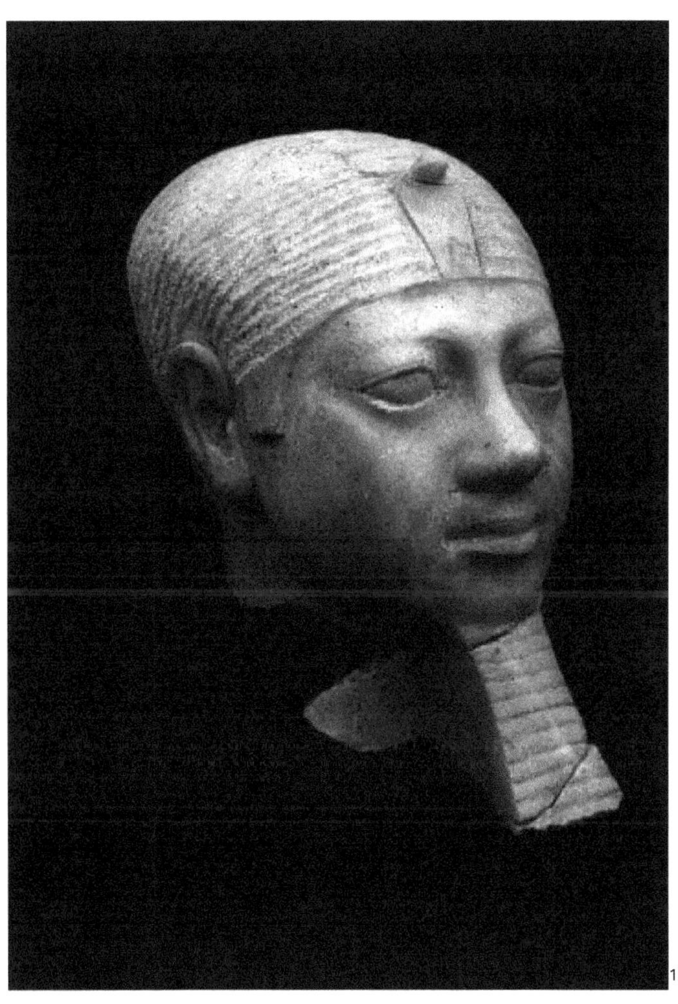

[18]

[18] All Photos were compiled by Brother Okomfo Nkuu Apem and The Metropolitan Museum of Art (1999). _Egyptian Art in the Age of the Pyramids_, Harry N. Abrams, Inc. New York, NY.

When it comes to our sisters, we all know many that have hair style like the picture below, but many don't know that these are traditional hairstyles, and some even belong to certain deities or towns. Below are hair styles of the Yorùbá people.

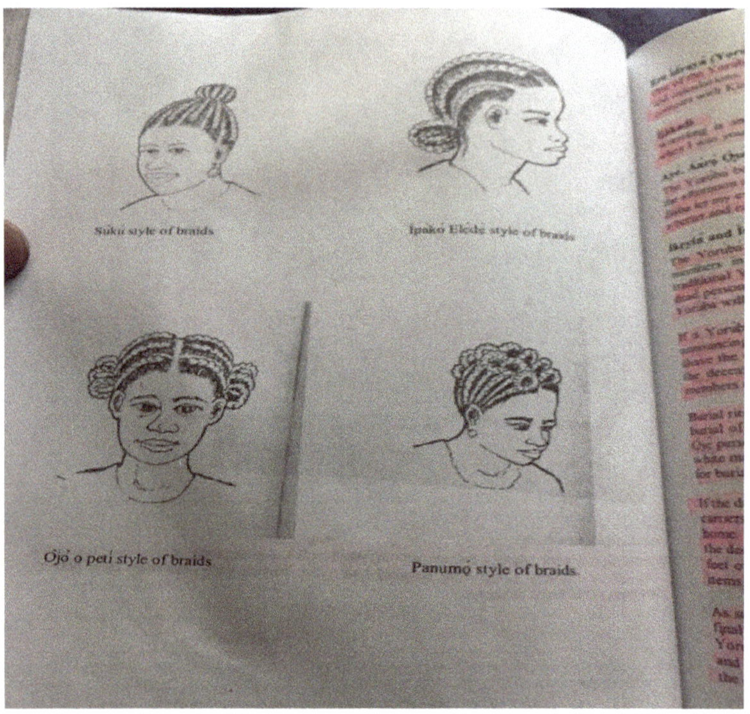

Our sisters were very instrumental in helping us escape slavery once we were in bondage in the diaspora. They used their hairstyles to lead us to freedom. When one thinks of corn rolls today they may think of west coast gangsters or Allen Iverson but there is a rich history behind this hair style. Depictions of women with cornrows have been found in Stone Age paintings in the Tassili Plateau of the Sahara, and have been dated as far back as 3000 B.C. There are also Native American paintings as far back as 1,000 years showing cornrows as a hairstyle. This tradition of female styling in cornrows has remained popular throughout Africa, particularly in the Horn of Africa and West Africa.[19] With this particular style our sisters used cornrows to transfer and create maps to leave plantations and the home of their captors. This act of using hair as a tool for resistance is said to have been evident across South America. It is most documented in Colombia where Benkos Bioho, a King captured from Africa by the Portuguese who escaped slavery, built San Basilio de Palenque, a village in Northern Colombia around the 17thcentury. Bioho created his own language as well as intelligence network and also came up with the idea to have women create maps and deliver messages through their cornrows.[20] Over time people generations later adopted this style of braids to honor their heritage and exhibit small acts of rebellion, this is the principal philosophy behind dread locks as well. If one had dreadlocks at a certain time period it

---

[19] https://face2faceafrica.com/article/how-cornrows-were-used-as-an-escape-map-from-slavery-across-south-america

[20] https://edtimes.in/africans-used-to-hide-escape-maps-from-slavery-in-their-hairstyles/

meant that person was symbolically saying they were for the rejection of Babylon and a refusal to conform to its norms regarding grooming aesthetics. Our community of memory has been somewhat fractured so today we wear these styles without the knowledge of their historical significance.

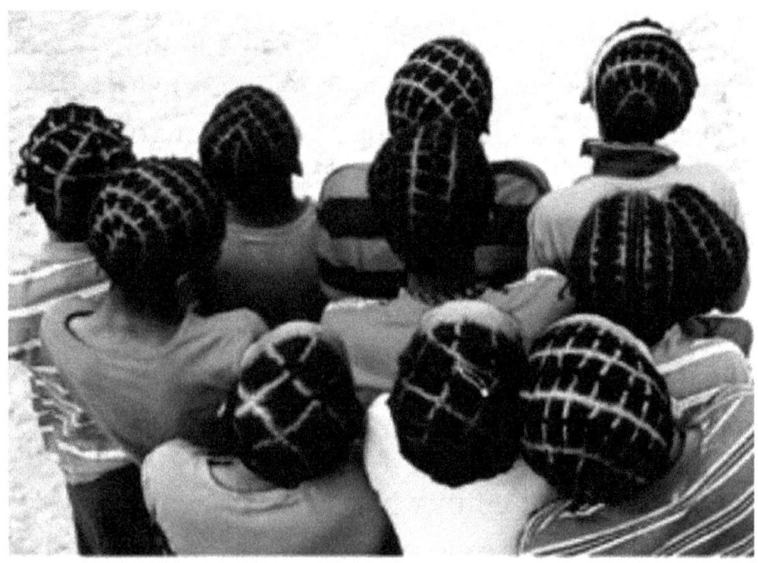

The Ekoi people of Ibibo land in Nigeria and Cameroon who are also called the leopard people due to their Ki.môyo called Ekpe have various hairstyle that also mirror styles we see today.

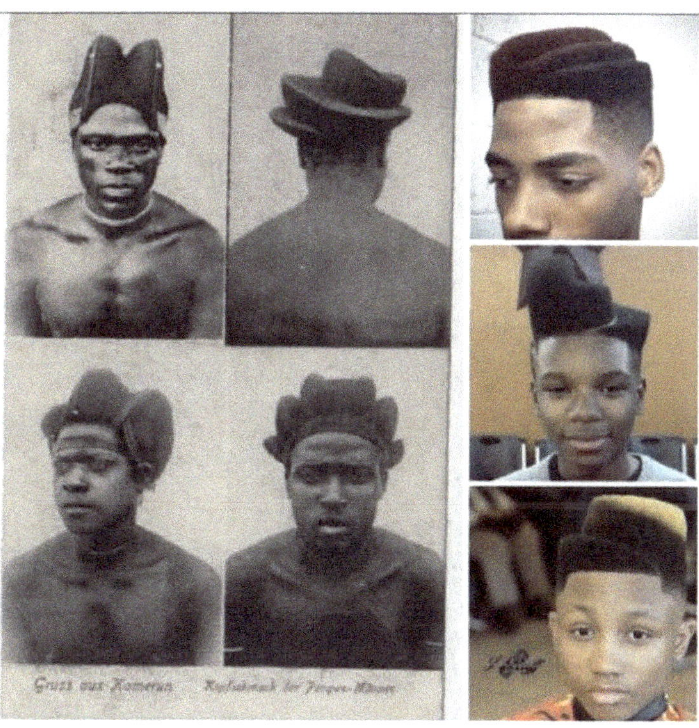

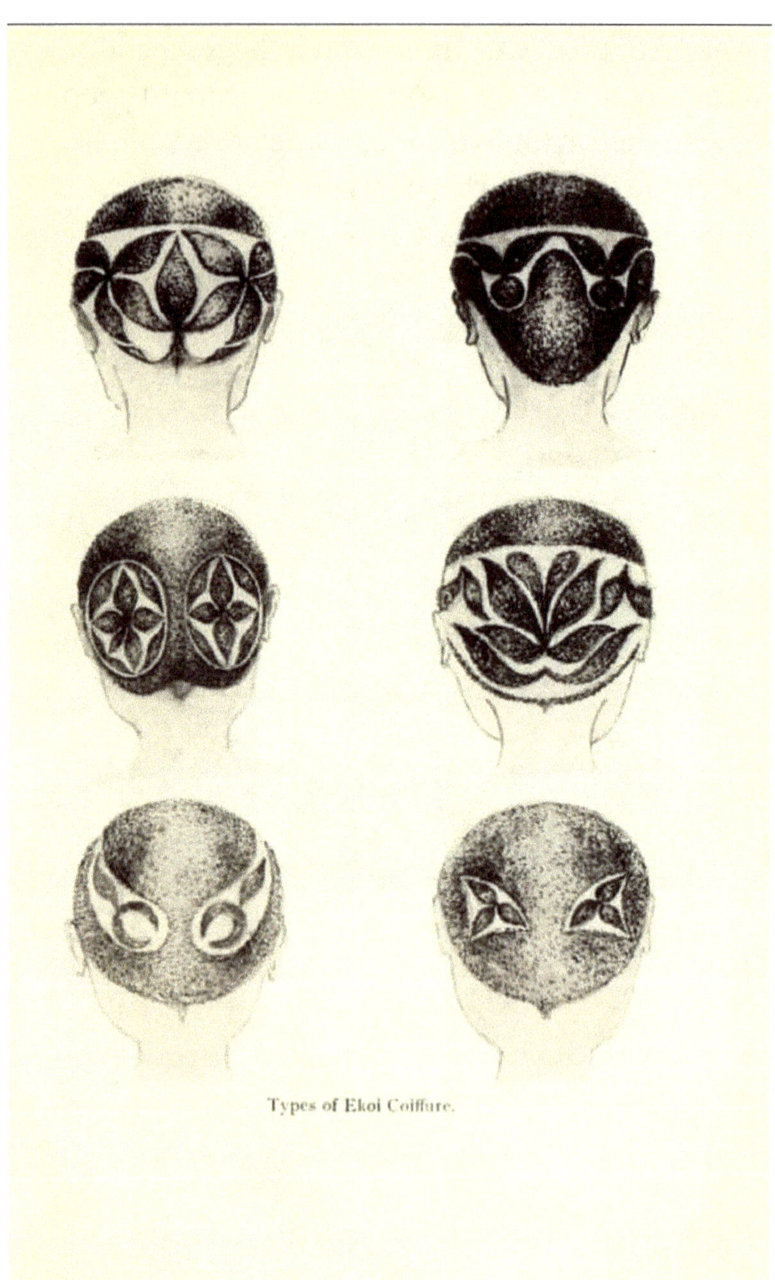

Types of Ekoi Coiffure.

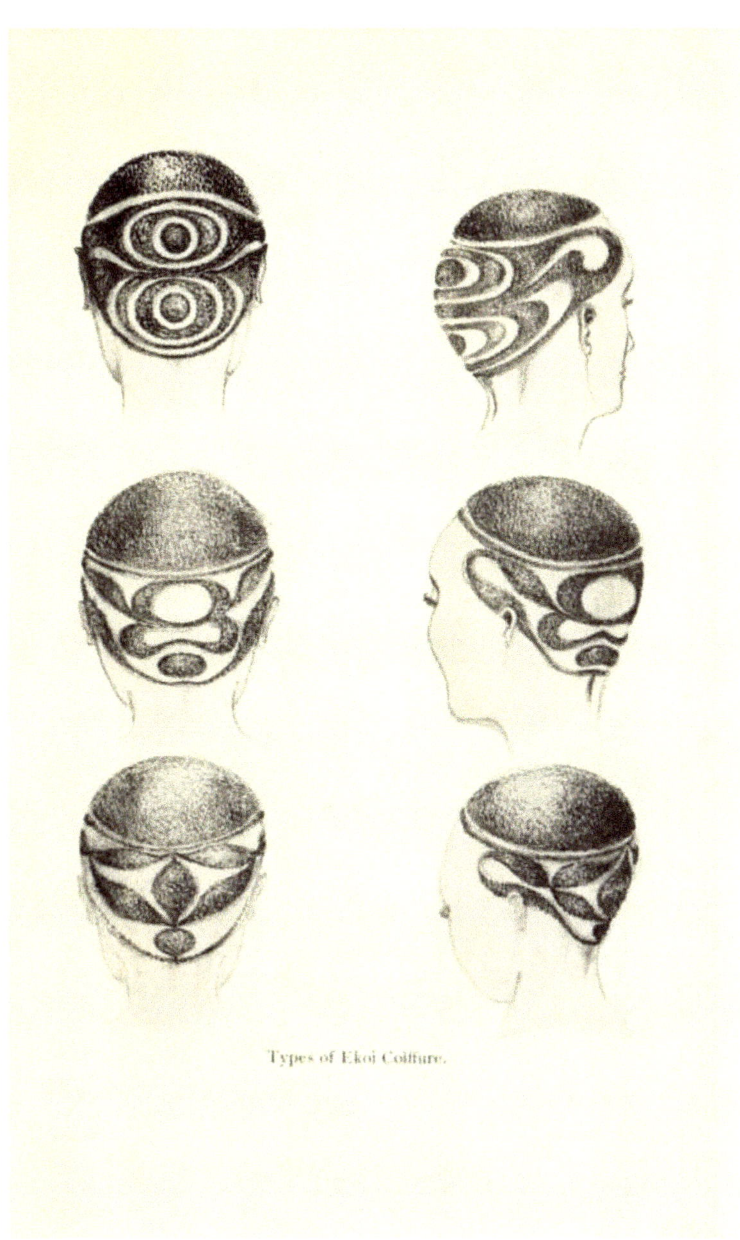

Types of Ekoi Coiffure.

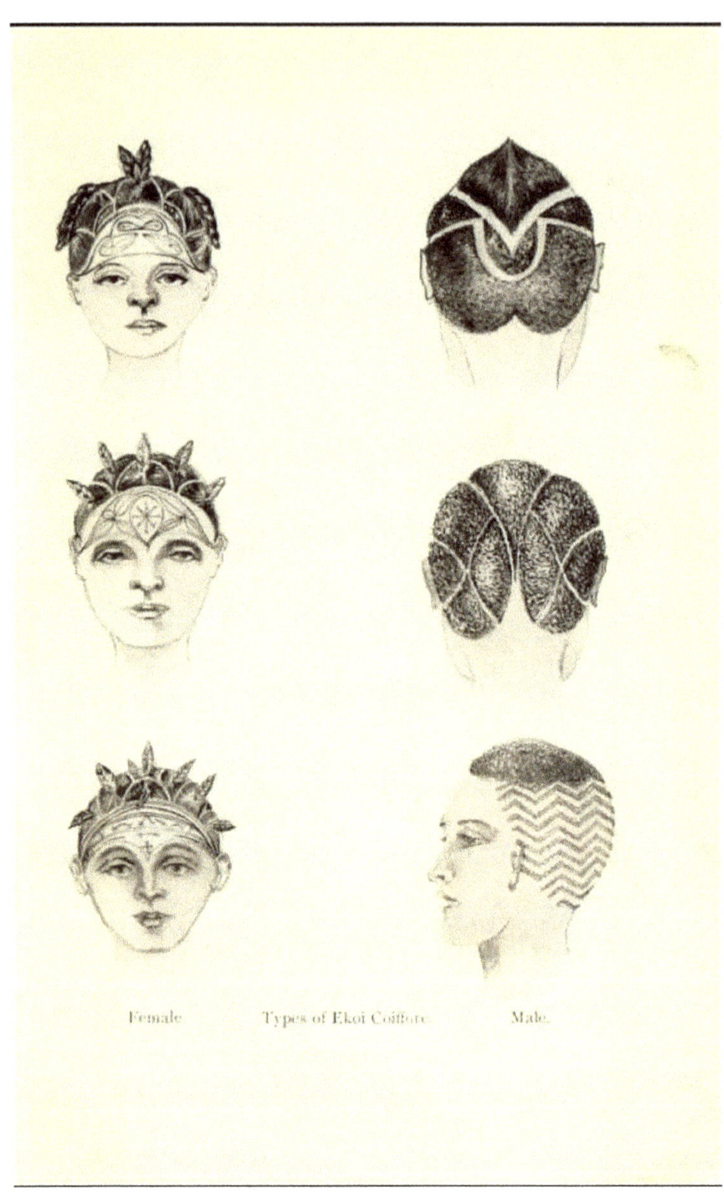

Female. Types of Ekoi Coiffure. Male.

Before I close this section out I must all mention a practice we Afrikans in America engage in that comes directly from our Ki.môyo. The practice of hiding or burning hair. The old saying is burning your hair or hide your hair before the birds get it and make you crazy. You will also hear don't let anyone get your hair. These old saying correlate directly with the spiritual traditions of Afrika. In Benin and Nigeria amongst the traditions of Isese and Vodun it is a common practice to hide or burn your hair because they can be used in many rituals for one to set themselves against a person. They are also used in healing medicinal rituals as well. There are even some deities made with one's hair to bind that deity to the lineage of the hair it belongs to. Once again, the community of memory rears his head in Afrikan in the diaspora practices.

Jazz Afrikan Connection

Jazz is a music genre that originated in the African American communities of New Orleans, Louisiana, United States, in the late 19th and early 20th centuries, with its roots in blues and ragtime.[21] Jazz has its roots in West Afrika and new traditions Afrikans in America cultivated.[22] From the very beginning in the New Orleans Jazz circuit Afrika was at the forefront. It should be no surprise that in the 1800's the popular jazz spot was called Congo Square. Congo Square was a place where enslaved Afrikans use to congregate and play the music they knew to play from their community of memory. This music was the foundation for what we know as jazz music today. Common instruments were the drums, gourds and banjolike instruments, all of these instruments can be found to this day in west Afrika.[23] Congo Square was also a spiritual place where Afrikan people could practice their ki.môyo. Mainly west Afrikan Vodú was practiced here and that in how New Orleans became a place known for Vodú.[24] It

---

[21] Jazz Origins in New Orleans – New Orleans Jazz National Historical Park". National Park Service. Retrieved March 19, 2017.

[22] Ferris, Jean (1993) America's Musical Landscape. Brown and Benchmark. ISBN 0-697-12516-5. pp. 228, 233.

[23] American Slavery, Penguin History, paperback edition, 47 Peter Kolchin,

[24] Johnson, J. (1991). New Orleans's Congo Square: An Urban Setting for Early Afro-American Culture Formation. Louisiana History: The

is said that the music they were playing blended with European and other types of music. The rhythmic call and response style found new homes inside of other instruments and flavor. An 1885 account says that they were making strange music (Creole) on an equally strange variety of 'instruments'—washboards, washtubs, jugs, boxes beaten with sticks or bones and a drum made by stretching skin over a flour-barrel.[25] During this time there were laws called the black codes these were laws governing the conduct of Afrikans in America whether they were enslaved or not. So, the reason why you see these seemingly primitive instruments was due to the fact that drumming was outlawed under the black codes. This meant Afrikan drumming traditions were not preserved in North America, unlike in Cuba, Haiti, and elsewhere in the Caribbean. African-based rhythmic patterns were retained in the United States in large part through "body rhythms" such as stomping, clapping, and patting juba dancing.[26] This rhythmic style also is a part of what we now know as Jazz. Muhal Richard Abrams who was a Jazz pianist and free Jazz medium, he helped

---

Journal of the Louisiana Historical Association, 32(2), 117-157. Retrieved April 20, 2021, from http://www.jstor.org/stable/4232877

[25] "On the Instrumental Origins of Jazz". American Quarterly Roth, Russell (1952). 4 (4): 305–16. doi:10.2307/3031415. ISSN 0003-0678. JSTOR 3031415.

[26] Palmer, Robert (1981). Deep Blues. New York: Viking. p. 37

launch the Association for the Advancement of Creative Musicians in 1965. The AACM blended elements of modern classical music with traditional African styles, while rejecting the notion of commercially palatable music.[27] He spoke often about the Jazz and Afrikan music connection and on the cover of his song Mama and Daddy he is dressed in traditional Malian Afrikan attire. John Carter an American jazz clarinet, saxophone, and flute player also expressed the African Jazz connection on the cover of his album covers (see picture). Between 1982 and 1990 Carter composed and recorded Roots and Folklore: Episodes in the Development of American Folk Music, five albums focused on African Americans and their history.[28] Jazz is a Afrikan black creation and many of its heights were achieved by Afrikan people. If we were to tap into the origins of the mechanisms that make Jazz we would further strengthen our spiritual and cultural power.

---

[27] https://www.washingtonpost.com/local/obituaries/muhal-richard-abrams-pianist-who-expanded-the-limits-of-jazz-dies-at-87/2017/11/02/dccae754-bfdc-11e7-97d9-bdab5a0ab381_story.html
[28] https://jazz.fandom.com/wiki/John_Carter_(jazz_musician)

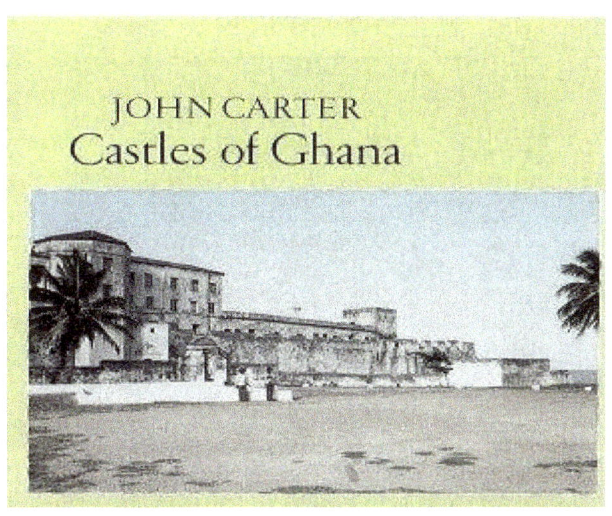
JOHN CARTER
Castles of Ghana

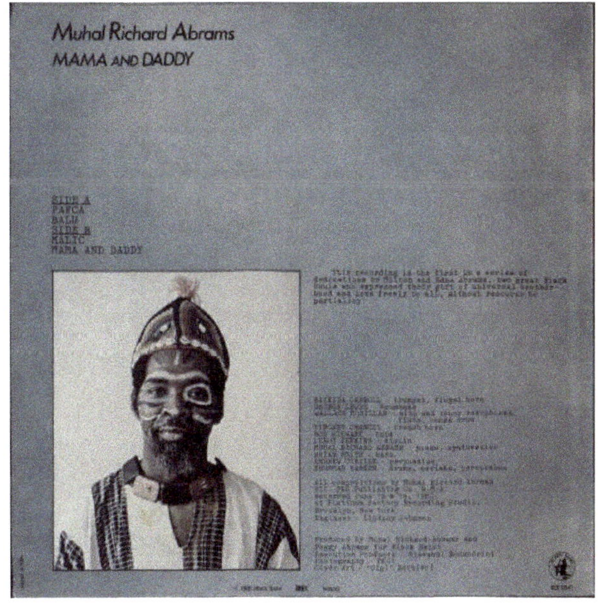
Muhal Richard Abrams
MAMA AND DADDY

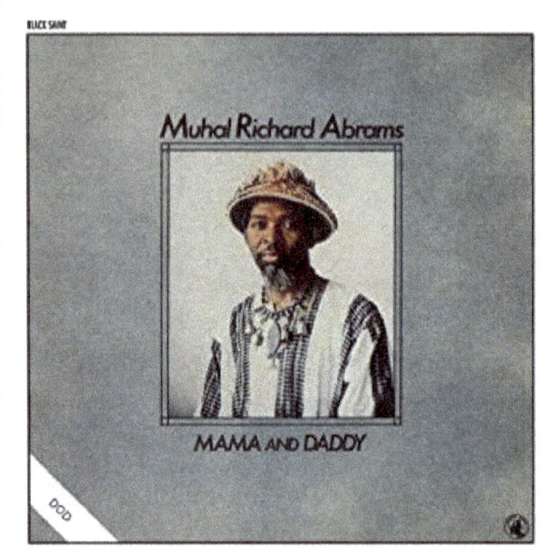
BLACK SAINT
Muhal Richard Abrams
MAMA AND DADDY
DOD

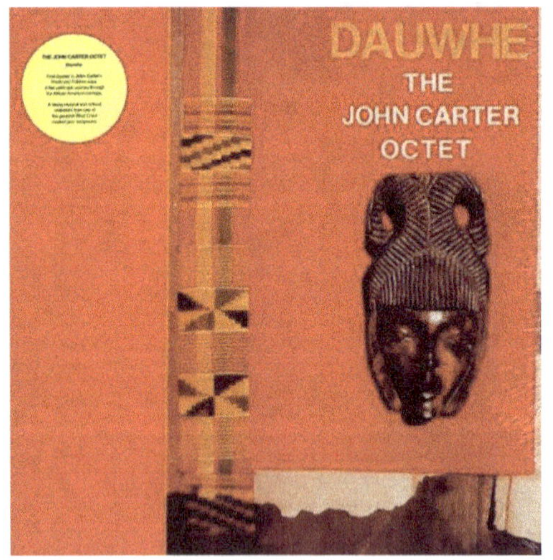
DAUWHE
THE
JOHN CARTER
OCTET

Waist Beads

Waist beads is something that has become very popular in the last 5 years or so. Models, rappers, dancers, strippers, and even just everyday regular women have started wearing Afrikan waist beads for a variety of reasons. Many people are aware that they have their roots in Afrika, but they are not aware of the specifics. They are also not aware that even though the practice has surged in popularity this is not the first time Afrikan people in America has dawned waist beads. There is a little debate about waist beads Afrikan origins but from what we can analyze waist beads origin in Afrika points to ancient KMT (Egypt). The Journal of Archeological Science reported that in 2013 5,000 years old Egyptian iron beads made from hammered meteoritic iron were discovered amongst 277 burials dated by ceramic and other finds to Naqada Period phases IIC to IIIA, or in terms of absolute chronology about 3400–3100 BC.[29] A total of nine tubular iron beads were retrieved from the cemetery, all from two closed archaeological contexts, and so of secure date. Seven were recorded in tomb 67: three from the waist of the deceased, and four as part of a necklace placed round his neck (Petrie et al., 1912:

---

29 https://www.sciencedirect.com/science/article/pii/S0305440313002057

15–16). The necklace beads were found in their original order as strung with tubular lapis lazuli, carnelian, agate, and gold beads. Petrie et al. (1912: pl. IV.2) present the necklace beads in order as found; UC10742 is the modern restringing in a different order and excluding the iron beads (see pic below).[30] These beads seem to be some type of adornment and I have not found evidence to specify why. We do know beads made its way to west Afrika. In West Africa, many historians believe the tradition of waist beads was popularized by the Yorùbá tribes, notably in Senegal and Ghana (notably the Ewes, Ashantis, Krobos, Ga-Adangbes) where they speak of nobility, femininity, and affluence. Today, countries like Ivory Coast and Sierra Leone have also adopted the waist bead.[31] The archeological site known as Igbo-Ukwu was a was clearly a burial place for an elite (wealthy) person, buried with a large array of grave goods, but it is unknown whether this person was a ruler or had some other religious or secular role in his or her community. The principal interment is an adult seated on a wooden stool, dressed in fine clothing

---

[30] W.M.F. Petrie, G.A. Wainwright, E. Mackay
The Labyrinth, Gerzeh and Mazghuneh, vol. XXI, British School of Archaeology in Egypt, London (1912)

[31] https://answersafrica.com/the-african-waist-beads-significance-and-uses.html

and with rich grave effects including over 150,000 glass beads. The remains of five attendants were found alongside. The burial included a number of elaborate cast bronze vases, bowls, and ornaments, made with the lost wax (or lost latex) technique. Elephant tusks and bronze and silver objects illustrated with elephants were found. The bronze pommel of a sword hilt in the form of a horse and rider was also found in this burial, as were wooden objects and vegetable textiles preserved by their proximity to bronze artifacts.[32] In Ghana waist beads powder glass waist beads have been documented as a part of their culture. The enlistment of beads' generative powers in the promotion of human fertility is a long-standing custom throughout southern Ghana.[33] A creative response to challenges of late- twentieth century transcultural engagements, painted beads provide a sustainable, locally produced bead form capable of satisfying the needs of customary practice as bead regalia for traditional rulers and Krobo nobility displays, as well as funerary presentations of waist beads honoring a deceased Asante woman (see pic below).[34] Once again, we see beads in Afrikan

---

[32] https://www.thoughtco.com/igbo-ukwu-nigeria-site-171378

[33] Ghana's Glass Beadmaking Arts in Transcultural Dialogues By Suzanne Gott

[34] Ghana's Glass Beadmaking Arts in Transcultural Dialogues By Suzanne Gott

culture adorning a deceased woman, from my observation this denotes importance and status in Ghana and in KMT. Beads take on a spiritual meaning as well in many Afrikan cultures. According to Akan oral traditions, the origins of two of Ghana's major historical powers are traced to the sacred stools of precious beads or gold that descended from the heavens, containing the spiritual essence of their peoples. For the Asante, the very "soul" (sunsum) of their nation resides in Sika Dwa Kofi, the Golden Stool "born on a Friday." For the Denkyira, whose political power preceded that of Asante, the most sacrosanct of royal regalia was Abankamdwa, the Stool of Precious Beads, which had the capacity to "call down a whirl- wind" when moved without the performance of the required customary rites. The regalia of Adanse, the Akan state located at the mythic center of Akan creation, includes a royal orator's staff called AhweneE Nana, "Great Ancestral Bead". The staff finial depicts the Adanse ruler as a "grandchild of beads," enstooled upon a platform supported by the great bead ancestress of Adanse's ruling Ekoɔna matriclan. The ancestral bead is represented by a long powder-glass encased iron rod, suspended from a carved head. The powder-glass is embellished with characteristic bead designs of trailed glass Abɔdɔm (sg.bɔdɔm) is the Akan name for the most precious reproductively powerful beads, with the Ekoɔna clan's bead ancestress an especially powerful bɔdɔm bead.[35] We now can properly deduce why waist beads are important in Ghana's culture and we see different beads had different meanings. The Yorùbá people of Southwestern Nigeria also have a longstanding tradition with waist beads. They are worn for protection and for help with losing weight. The practicality still amazes me to this day. A waist bead will be made and placed on a person, if the waist bead becomes loose then they are losing weight and if it gets tight or burst then that person is not meeting their weight goals, such ingenuity in classical Afrika societies is usually not mentioned in most books. In the Yorùbá society men and women where waist beads. Depending on color the beads can also be tied to specific deities. They are called ileke and they also encircle and guard other major points where parts of the body to include wrist, waist, ankles.[36] Women's Yorùbá waist beads are known as bebe are known to serve erotic functions and have the power to attract and evoke deep emotional responses[37] which is not different from modern day uses. Our community of

[35] Ghana's Glass Beadmaking Arts in Transcultural Dialogues by Suzanne Gott

[36] Yorùbá Beadwork in the Americas: Òrìsà and Bead Color by John Mason

[37] Drewal, H. (1998). Yorùbá Beadwork in Africa. African Arts, 31(1), 18-94. doi:10.2307/3337620

memory has seemly retained this purpose and resurrected it in modern times. How we have retained this cultural practice is something that many people may not be aware of. Often the community of memory arguments is used but the time period is rarely annotated correctly. Enslaved and free Afrikans in the southeastern United Sates used beads to participate in a shared identity that has its origins in Afrikan traditions. The majority of these beads were made of glass, and most were blue, white and clear color. At the archeological site 38GE560 which was occupied from the early 18th to 20th century excavations uncovered multiple beads of multiple types. These beads were used as cultural identifiers for their ancestral homeland.[38] Blue beads are consistent finds at African American sites. Archaeologists acknowledge these artifacts were used for adornment, yet some researchers also propose beads possessed additional cultural meaning among African Americans. For this study bead data from African American sites in the South are analyzed. The results indicate blue is the predominant bead color. The prevalence of these items suggests they may

---

[38] Dillian, C. (2011). COLONOWARE BEAD PRODUCTION AND AFRICAN AMERICAN TRADITION AT 38GE560, GEORGETOWN COUNTY, SOUTH CAROLINA. Archaeology of Eastern North America, 39, 53-65. Retrieved May 15, 2021, from http://www.jstor.org/stable/23265114

indeed have been an important yet unrecognized aspect of African American culture. The multiple underlying meanings assigned to blue beads are considered through reference to ethnographic information, folklore, and oral history associated with West and Central Africa and the Southeast.[39] There is a place of great importance in New York City called the Afrikan Burial Ground Monument. Here in this sacred place lies the remains of up to 20,000 Afrikans of enslaved and free from the 1700 time period. Found at this site were a total of 148 beads representing 14 varieties from seven burials: Burial 107, Burial 187, Burial 226, Burial 250, Burial 340, Burial 428, and Burial 434. The majority of the 148 beads (113 beads representing eight varieties) were recovered from a single burial, Burial 340. One hundred forty-six of the 148 beads were glass, one was bone, and one was amber.[40] This is why I titled this chapter returning to a practice we already engage in. We are already doing some of the work to preserve this culture without realizing it.

---

[39] ADAMS, NATALIE 1993 Archaeological Investigations at 38GE377: Examination of a Deep Creek Phase Site and a Portion of the Eighteenth-Century Midway Plantation. Research Series 37. Chicora Foundation, Columbia, South Carolina

[40] THE ARCHEOLOGY OF 290 BROADWAY VOLUME IV CONSERVATION OF MATERIALS FROM THE AFRICAN BURIAL GROUND AND THE NON-MORTUARY CONTEXTS

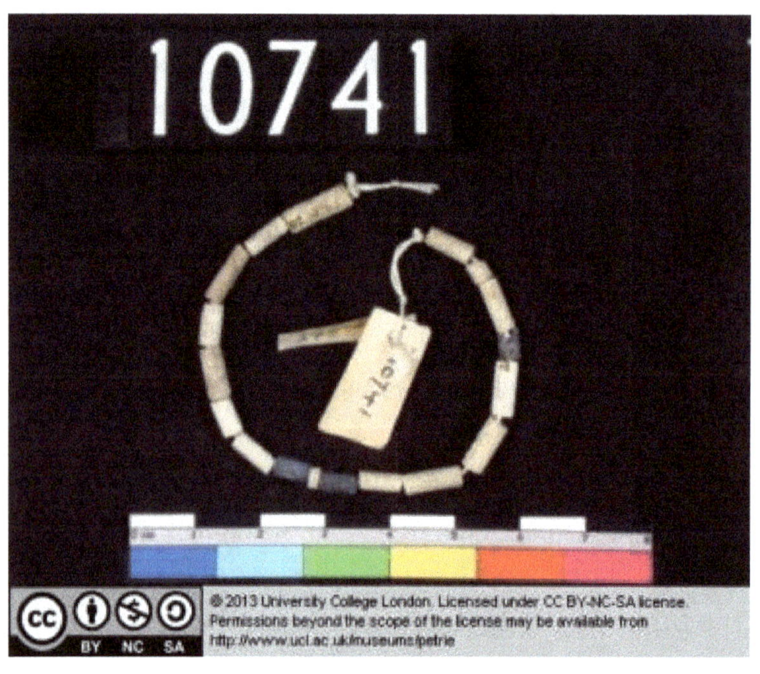
10741
© 2013 University College London. Licensed under CC BY-NC-SA license.
Permissions beyond the scope of the license may be available from
http://www.ucl.ac.uk/museums/petrie

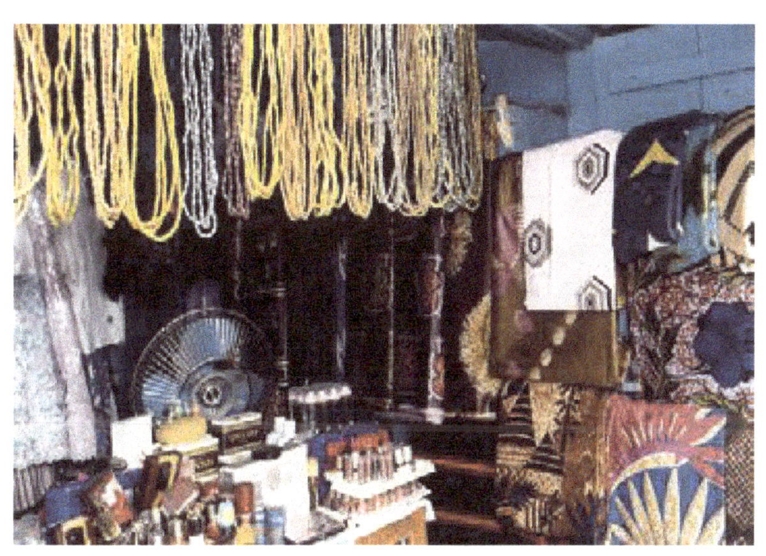

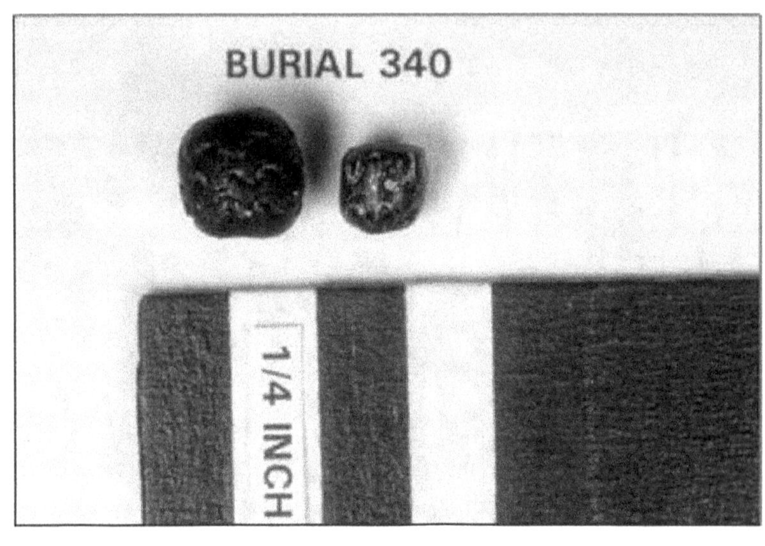
BURIAL 340
1/4 INCH

Libation Rituals

This is a practice I'm sure a lot of black people have seen but don't know of its importance. In every Afrikan spiritual tradition or ki.môyo I have studied there is an element of libation. Libation is a ritual act of prayer, worship and praise for a divinity or ancestor in liquid form. Water, gin, and palm wine are some of the liquids use for this action. For instance, a libation in the form of drinks is poured to venerate and invoke the blessing of family ancestors on behalf of the newborn baby. This symbolic presentation of drinks or sometimes food to the ancestors is a token of fellowship, hospitality, and respect. Libations are also symbols of family continuity and contact, which coincide with the announcement and blessing of the child's names.[41] In the festival of Adae amongst the Akan when entering the Nkonuafieso (shrine room), thc priest greets the ancestors by calling each of their names, one by one, and offering them each a drink through libation. Amongst the Ga people in Ghana during their harvest festival a meal is prepared for their ancestors and libations are given in their memory. Amongst the Haitians in Haitian Voodoo, it is thought that those that neglect libations and have come for a far journey will encounter misfortune

[41] Molefi Asante and Ama Azama Encyclopedia of African Religion

on their way back. The Bamana tradition of Mali says libations must be poured to them regularly, especially before consulting with or requesting something from the ancestors. We can see from these examples that libation is an Afrikan practice so naturally we find this same practice amongst Afrikans in America. How many times have you seen brothers says "I'm gonna pour some out for the dead homies" or "this shot is for my brothers". Where did we get that act from? It certainly wasn't taught to us in slavery. This too is a part of the community of memory knowledge that we have retained. Libation is a ritual we engage in all the time, and it is an essential part of our Afrikan essence.

Carnival

Those of us black Afrikan folks that have Caribbean influence in our families know about carnival. Whether it be in Trinidad, Belize, Uruguay, or Colombia there is an Afrikan historical narrative that is rarely told about carnival. First let me say that carnival is a masquerade by definition. Afrikan people have been exhibiting masquerade for centuries. The Chiwara masquerades of Mali are often organized at the beginning of a new planting season to ensure a good harvest. The Bamilike people of Cameroon have masquerades symbolizing ancestral spirits and magical statues are common artifacts used within the kingdoms. These artifacts, including skulls of deceased ancestors and musical equipment xylophones, drums, and flutes are kept in a secret place in the home of the eldest living male in each lineage. The Yorùbá have an annual Egungun festival in which is a masquerade begins under the direction of a family elder or Alagba, the society feels a strong bond with the ancestors because they realize that the Egungun will help them invoke the powers of their great ancestors through drumming and dance. The masquerades organized by the Eastern Igbo as part of their harvest festival are also well documented. The Ogoni from Nigeria have also commonly celebrated the harvest of yams with masked dances. The Senufo people of the Ivory Coast have a masquerade in which the designs, regarded as protective, are painted onto locally woven narrow strip cloth using green paint made from boiled leaves, then outlined with a mud solution.[42] These Afrikan masquerades are the basis for the carnival masquerades you see today. Let's look at some historical narratives. In Belize they have Comparsas which are masqueraders.They consist of large groups of dancers dancing and traveling on the streets followed by a Carrosa (carriage) where the musicians play. The Comparsa is a development of African processions where groups of devotees follow a given saint or deity during a particular religious celebration.[43] In Uruguay European archetypes such as Pierrot, Harlequin, and Columbina merge with African ancestral elements such as The Old Mother or Mama Vieja, the Medicine Man or Gramillero and the Magician or Escobero in their carnival festival.[44] These are well documented influences that are usually not

---

[42] Molefi Asante and Ama Azama Encyclopedia of African Religion

[43] Sands, R. (1991). Carnival Celebrations in Africa and the New World: Junkanoo and the Black Indians of Mardi Gras. Black Music Research Journal, 11(1), 75-92. doi:10.2307/779245

[44] Gittens, William Anderson (2019). Culture Demystify A Cultural Conversation First. Devgro Media Arts Services. pp. 374–375. ISBN 9789769635616.

discussed. Let’s look at a Carnival costume and an Egúngún costume from Nigeria.

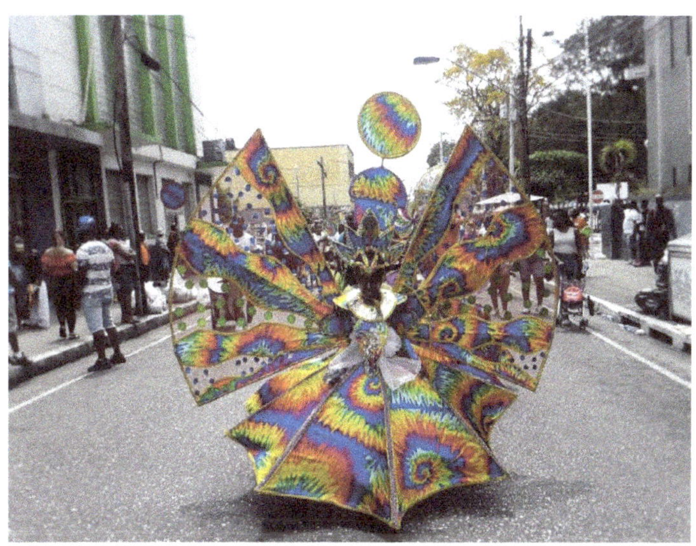

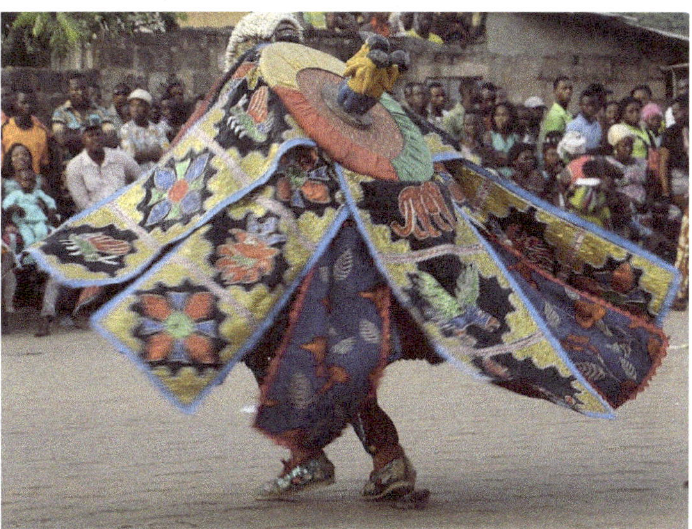

You can see how these masquerades are very similar and how much influence the costumes of carnival have retained from the Afrikans. There is another performer we have not talked about that is present at carnival as well. The Trindadian and Tobagan carnival have a performer called the Moko Jumbi commonly known as a stilt walker. These performers achieve the impossible task of a balancing act while entertaining the crowd. The original Moko Jumbie was a spirit dancer from West Afrika. "Moko" is a West African word that refers to gods and "Jumbie" means ghost. Stilt walkers Moko jumbie where spiritual beings that could see high for medicine and spot evil. In West Africa, Moko Jumbies are known to kidnap and eat disobedient children, steal dreams and see into evildoers' hearts and terrorize them. They walk through villages on 10- to 15-foot-high stilts wearing the traditional skirt of palm leaves and woven grass, and a pointed headdress that covers the face. The Moko Jumbie crossed the sea on the slave ships of the 1800s. The Mandinkas, Igbo, Okpolo, and Cote D'Ivore all had these types of masquerades in West Afrika[45]. The Moko Jumbie tradition remains strong in the Caribbean. The Moko Jumbie that came loping down the road is

---

[45] Nicholls, R. (1999). The Mocko Jumbie of the U.S. Virgin Islands; History and Antecedents. African Arts, 32(3), 49-96. doi:10.2307/3337709

from the Caribbean's myriad cultures, which influenced the vibrant costumes and musical hats. Sometimes Moko Jumbies wear masks or makeup.[46] Females wear beautiful head wraps and long, flowing skirts over satin leggings. Let's take a look at these wonderful masquerades.

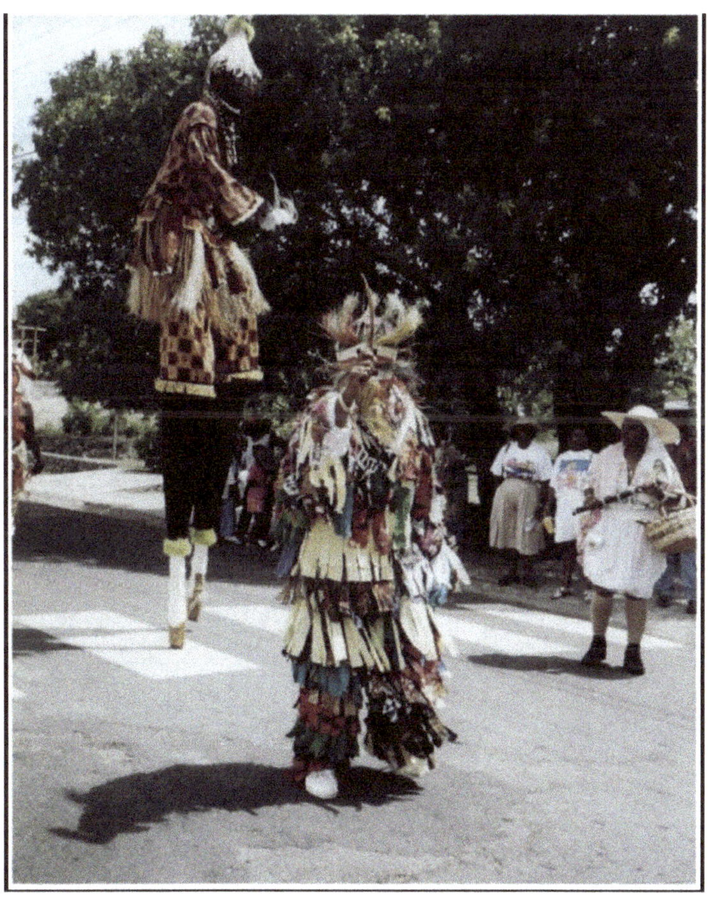

[46]https://eric.ed.gov/?id=EJ856240

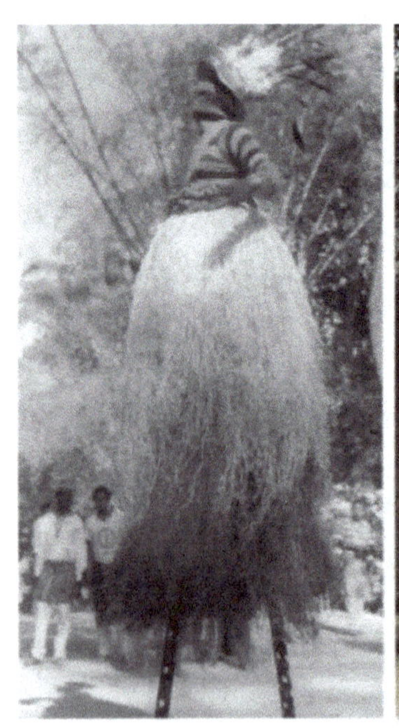
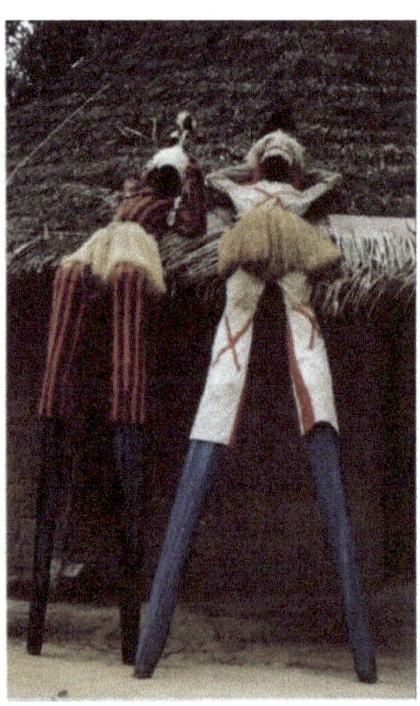

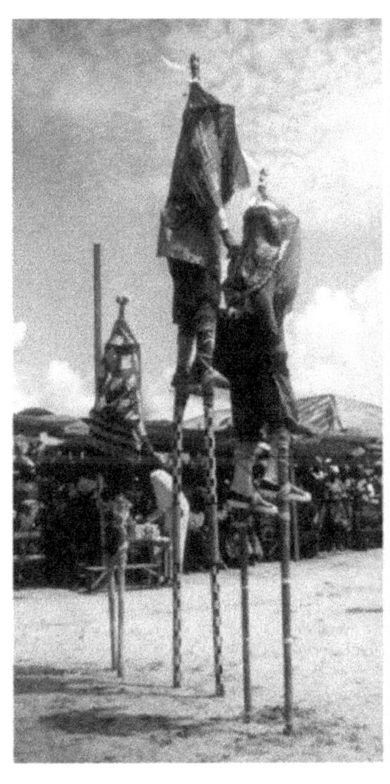

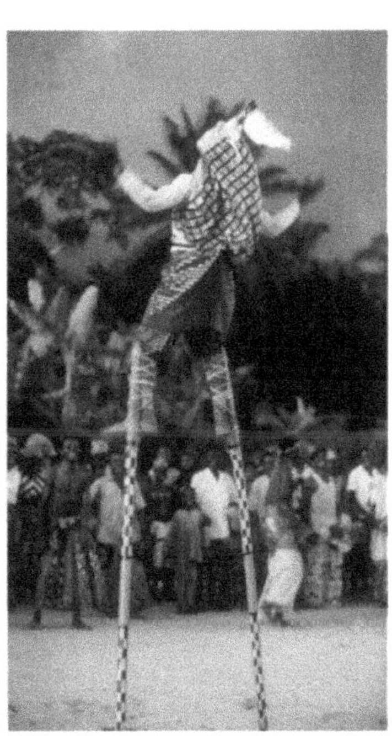

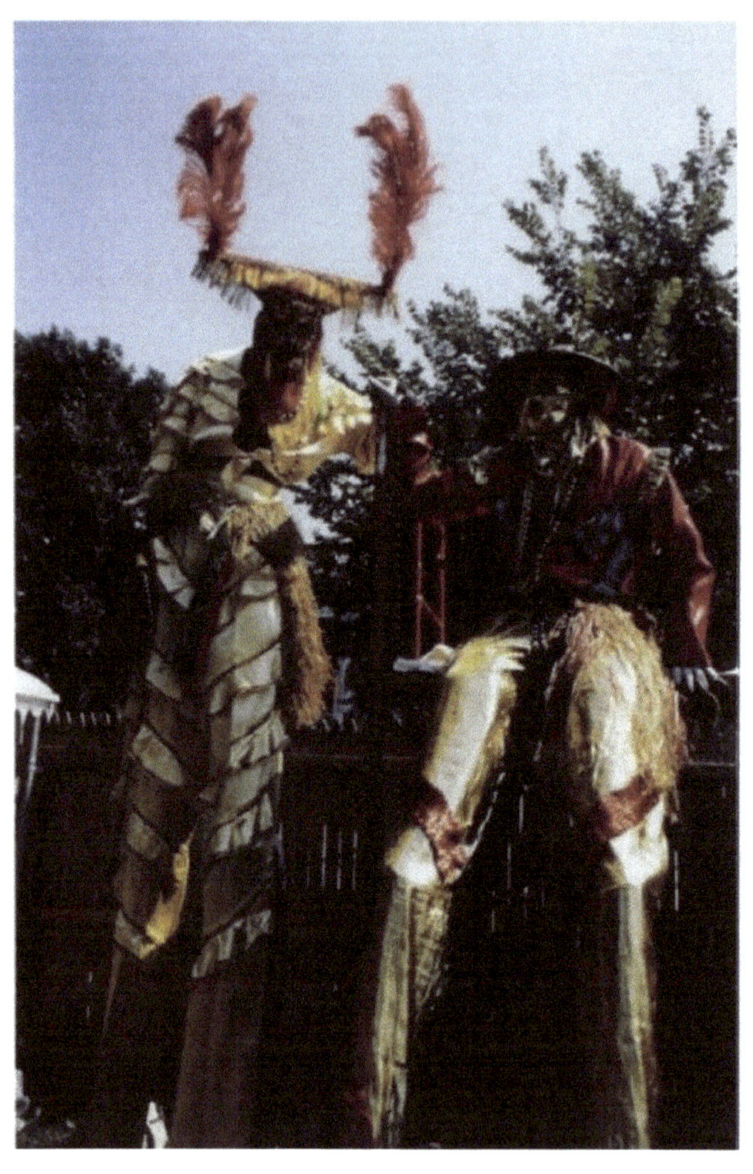

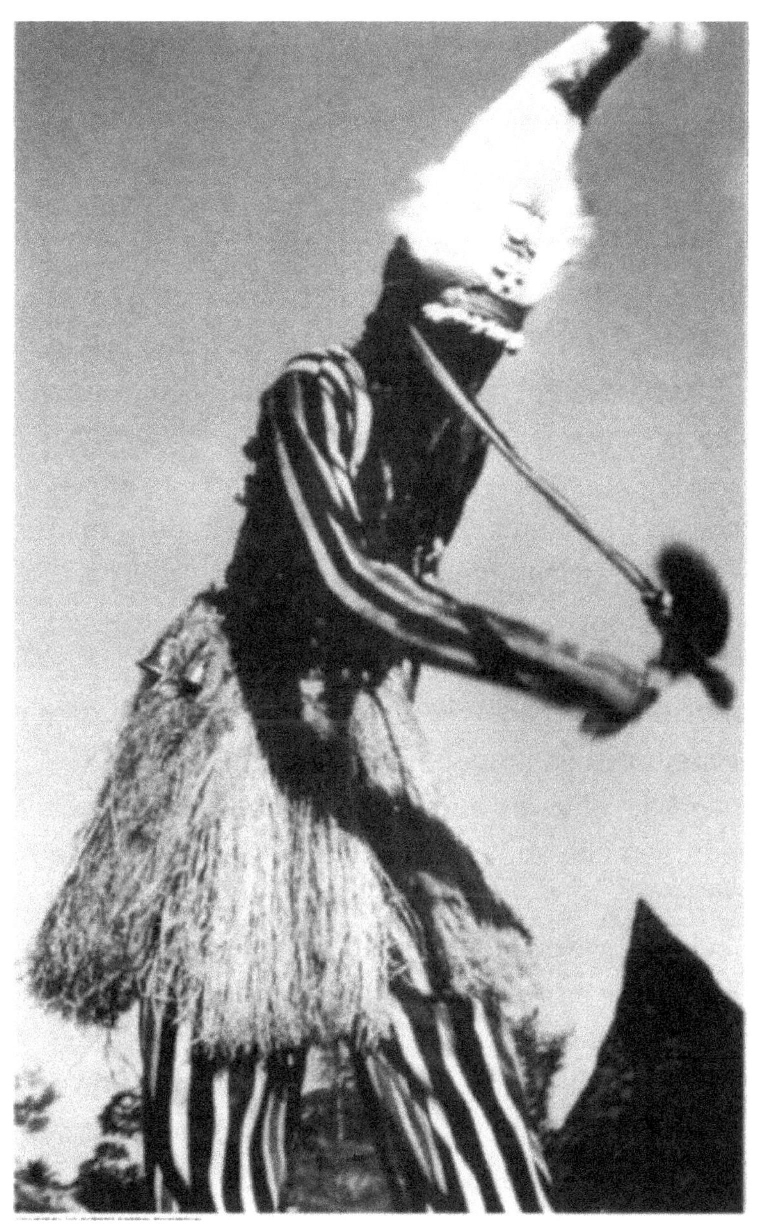

Susu and Cooperative Economics

There is a classical Afrikan concept called Susu which made its way to the Caribbean and the United States by Afrikan slaves. Susu or Sou-sou, which comes from the Yorùbá term "esesu," originated in West Africa, but is practiced in many African and Caribbean countries. Over the years, sou-sou has evolved, but the basic concept remains the same. Somalis call it "hagbad" or "ayuuto"; in Jamaica, it is known as a "partner"; in Guyana, a "box hand"; Haitians call it a "min"; and if you are Southern African, you may know it as "stokvel."[47] The concept works as such the group elects a treasurer who will collect the members contributions. She will also create a payout roster, or members can request to receive their hand at any given date during the cycle. Everyone agrees on how much and how often they want to contribute. If ten members are contributing $100 a week, each week a member will receive a $1,000 hand or cash lump sum. The cycle begins again after ten weeks. Any member who can afford it, can also double their contribution, and get paid two hands in one cycle.[48] Traditionally a council of elders would precede over all proceedings and if

---

[47] https://www.washingtoninformer.com/individuals-of-color-find-unique-savings-opportunities-with-sou-sou/

[48] https://www.washingtoninformer.com/individuals-of-color-find-unique-savings-opportunities-with-sou-sou/

there is any foul play divination would be consulted and punishments would be handed out. This concept is what black people have evolved into cooperative economics. Cooperative economics grew from mutual benefit and relief societies from the turn-of-the century when large numbers of immigrants from the Caribbean and migrants from the American South, made their way to urban areas like New York, Detroit, Boston, and St. Louis. With no official channel's city, state, or federal, in place to stabilize these quickly evolving communities, the newcomers banded together. Creating some of the nation's longest social services platforms, including the Trinidad Benevolent Association, the American West Indian Ladies Aid Society, and the Bermuda Benevolent Association, operated according to sociologist / author Ira De Augustine Reid for: mutual benefit and relief, economic and political adjustment in the U.S.; and the perpetuation of desirable conditions in their homelands. While the sou sou paid for mortgage and business down payments, other regular outings, literary forums, and gatherings paid out death and sick benefits to its members. Then, like now, the concept of collective or group economics and self-sacrifice remain central.[49] Our

[49] https://www.washingtoninformer.com/individuals-of-color-find-unique-savings-opportunities-with-sou-sou/

great brother and leader Marcus Garvey believed in economic independence for the African diaspora and through UNIA set about to achieve that through the formation of ventures like the Black Star Line and the Negro Factories Corporation.[50] Garvey understood there was no white salvation for the black man in America. He understood we had to do for self, that is the Susu spirit. Our great brother and leader Malcolm X understood the importance of this Afrikan concept. The concept of togetherness and solving our own problems. Malcolm said "Instead of the negro leaders having the black man begging for a chance to dine in white restaurants, the negro leaders should be showing the black man to do something to strengthen his own economy, to give himself an independent economy, or to provide job opportunities for himself. Not begging for a cup of coffee in a white man's restaurant."[51] Our great brother and leader Martin Luther King Jr. also understood the importance of cooperative economics. Martin said "You can't talk about solving the economic problem of the Negro without talking about billions of dollars, we are

---

[50] Chapman, Thandeka K. (2004). "Foundations of Multicultural Education: Marcus Garvey and the United Negro Improvement Association". The Journal of Negro Education.

[51] https://mises.org/power-market/malcolm-x-property-integration-and-economic-independence

treading in difficult waters, because it really means that we are saying that something is wrong… with capitalism. There must be a better distribution of wealth and maybe America must move toward a democratic socialism."[52] The foundation of democratic socialism is rooted is susu and although the concept is given to the British historically it's not hard to trace ideas of the philosophy to susu, the togetherness, the pulling together as a community and the power of election are Afrikan susu concepts. These three men set a susu foundational blueprint for many powerful movements in the future. The Black Panthers, The Nation of Islam, the Black Liberation Army, the Deacons of Defense, The New Black Panther party, The Organization of African Unity and even more. Today Susu's are still alive in Afrika and the diaspora. Organizations such as ULU (Us Lifting US) have drawn on these Afrikan susu systems for inspiration and expanded on the idea to reach a wider range of Afrikans in Amerika.

[52] https://mises.org/power-market/malcolm-x-property-integration-and-economic-independence

Dancing

Dancing for the Afrikan is more than moving to a rhythm or expressing approval when your favorite song comes on. It is ritual for us. It is one of the tools we use to connect and reconnect to that power which created and animates us, that Ase we each carry that can be used to unite entire communities and nations. In every single occasion of importance, we dance either here or on the continent. Where it's your uncles' barbeque or an initiation in Ghana, WE WILL DANCE! Today so many Afrikans in Amerika have become famous via social media for dance. The Tik Tok platform is popular because of dances young Afrikans from all over create. This is a tradition we carry in us from the continent. Allow me to illustrate what I mean. The people of Ghana have a spiritual tradition called Akom. The word Akom refers to dance.[53] "Akom is the general term given to a series of dances performed by the Akomfo. It is an intricate system of communication and healing that provides an opportunity for dancing to the specific cadences of religious drumming during what may be characterized as a spiritual gathering of the ancestors, the abosom, and the people gathered who sing, clap, drum, and dance." So important is this word that entire tradition can be named after it,

---

[53] Molefi Asante and Ama Azama Encyclopedia of African Religion

so important is this practice that it is used as a spiritual gathering of one's lineage, it is an intricate part of ritual and society as a whole. Another example is the [54] "Dogon in Mali, the use of dances for rain is attached to the majestic Dogon-Tellem figures that are known as "they who request of the spirits that the rain be released." The powerful ancestral figures are a collective prayer for rain. Singing and dancing around the figure, the priests are able to invoke the most archaic images in the land". So important that we use dance to call upon the rain in which we use for our subsentence and survival. We have forgotten the meaning behind dance in Amerika, but we never stopped dancing. Camile A brown has done extensive work in looking into over 25 dances by Afrikan people in Amerika and uncovering their origins. She talks about social dances emerging from communities. Remember the communities of memory in which I discussed earlier. We are remembering every time we dance, we are remembering from generations ago whether we know it or not.[55] Camile says in dance "the present always contains the past and the past shapes who we are and who we will be". The

---

[54] Molefi Asante and Ama Azama Encyclopedia of African Religion
[55] Camile A Brown
https://www.ted.com/talks/camille_a_brown_a_visual_history_of_social_dance_in_25_moves?fbclid=IwAR3ICj7X_MPmDoyGtM7kB5tCdh1gS9B86xb0ojyu32AmRgqUqMKxvszW6w0#t-54847

Juba dance is an example of an Afrikan dance that we did in Amerika as slave on the plantation. This dance helped us remember who we were. The Slave masters banned drumming on plantations, I believe they knew to some extent how special drumming was to us. We found a work around in this dance.[56] The dance is said to have come from the Kongo but just like the Yorùbá and Haitian drumming it communicates messages. Another dance that came from the congo is the popular dance from the 1950's called the Twist.[57] the Twist is popularized by Chubby Checker and Dick Clark. Suddenly, everybody's doing the Twist: white teenagers, kids in Latin America, making its way into songs and movies". There are many other dances that we do today that have Afrikan roots that we are just not aware of. Hence the point of this chapter, returning to something we already engage in. Which brings me to the most popular dance among Afrikan women

---

[56] Camile A Brown https://www.ted.com/talks/camille_a_brown_a_visual_history_of_social_dance_in_25_moves?fbclid=IwAR3ICj7X_MPmDoyGfM7kB5tCdh1gS9B86xb0ojyu32AmRgqUqMKxvszW6w0#t-54847

[57] https://www.ted.com/talks/camille_a_brown_a_visual_history_of_social_dance_in_25_moves?fbclid=IwAR3ICj7X_MPmDoyGfM7kB5tCdh1gS9B86xb0ojyu32AmRgqUqMKxvszW6w0#t-54847

in Amerika the twerk.[58] Twerking is a dance that arouse in the south of the United States in places like Louisiana, Atlanta, Memphis, Virginia Beach, Miami, and Houston. Twerking is defined as a type of dance that came out of the bounce music scene of New Orleans in the late 1980s. Individually performed chiefly but not exclusively by women, dancers move by throwing or thrusting their hips back or shaking their buttocks, often in a low squatting stance.[59][60][61] Once again, we must give credit to our family from the Kongo for the twerk. Twerking was called [62] kwassa kwassa is a dance created by Jeannora, a mechanic in Kinshasa from the Democratic Republic of the Congo, that started in the 1980s, where the hips move back and forth while the hands move to follow the hips. It was very popular in Africa.

---

[58] Holly, Hobbs (2012). "A Review of Matt Miller's Bounce: Rap Music and Local Identity in New Orleans". *Southern Spaces*. **2012**. doi:10.18737/M7ZC82.

[59] Miller, Matt (2012). *Bounce: Rap Music and Local Identity in New Orleans*. Boston: Univ of Massachusetts Press.

[60] "Twerk: Definition of Twerk in Oxford Dictionary - American English (US)". Oxford English Dictionary. Oxford University Press. Retrieved December 11, 2013.

[61] Dee, Jonathan (August 11, 2012). "Sissy Bounce, New Orleans's Gender-Bending Rap - NYTimes.com". *The New York Times*. Archived from the original on August 11, 2012. Retrieved June 30,2017.

[62] https://en.wikipedia.org/wiki/Kwassa_kwassa

The dance was popularized by soukous music videos, as well as the videos of Kanda Bongo Man, Pepe Kalle, Viva La Musica, and other Congolese musicians. For the first time in Congo, all the groups adopted these dance steps. This had not happened before because bands preferred to have their own specific dance.

We also must thank our family from Côte d'Ivoire for an even older version of the twerk called mapouka. Mapouka which means dance from behind is a dance from the Dabou area of southeast Côte d'Ivoire which is claimed to be a modernized version of a traditional dance originating from the Aizi, Alladian and Avikam people.[63] The dance is mostly performed by women, shaking their rear end side to side, facing away from their audience, often while bent over.[64] The Afrikan influence on today's dance scene is clear when studying it from its cultural context.

---

[63] Akindes, Simon (2002). "Playing it 'Loud and Straight': Reggae, Zouglou, Mapouka and Youth Insubordination in Côte d'Ivoire". *Playing with Identities in Contemporary Music in Africa*. Nordic Africa Institute. pp. 99–100. ISBN 9789171064967.

[64] Newell, Sasha (2012). The Modernity Bluff: Crime, Consumption, and Citizenship in Côte D'Ivoire. University of Chicago Press. p. 115. ISBN 978-0-226-57519-3.

Giving Dap

Afrikans in Amerika have a special way of greeting each other that many other races don't quite understand. We express our excitement to see one another with handshaking that isn't common in other cultures. It can be a smack, or end with a pop or even a dance at the end. Dap is a friendly gesture of greeting, agreement,
or solidarity between two people that has become popular in Western cultures, particularly since the 1970s, originating from African
American communities.[65] Scholars note that historically Black churches possessed secret handshakes, often called "giving skin" or "high fiving," which affirmed one's identity within the group. The complex handshakes associated with Black America have many names, including "soul shakes," "black power handshakes," or the "dap," each reflecting forms of nonverbal communication typically associated with Black GIs in Vietnam.[66]

It's become a regular form of expression among us and it's something we do without thinking and because of that fact we as Afrikans in Amerika probably haven't thought about it having an

---

[65] Dalzell, Tom (2009). The Routledge Dictionary of Modern American Slang and Unconventional English. Taylor & Francis. p. 271.

[66] https://www.aaihs.org/diasporic-salutations-and-the-west-african-origins-of-the-dap/

Afrikan root. Amongst the Igbo culture in Southeastern Nigeria if two speakers agreed with each other they would knock hands in the Igbo manner of clenching the fist and knocking it lightly against the fist of the person they're greeting. We can also look towards the Zulu culture in southern Afrika. While I was visiting Johannesburg, a man assumed I was a Zulu and started to do this certain handshake, once he realized I wasn't Zulu he said I looked like one and taught me this handshake. It's a three-part shake, beginning with a traditional handshake, shifting into an arm-wrestling position, and returning to the first position. It shocked me that this handshake was something me and my friends had done before but me and my friends had no idea we were doing a Zulu handshake. In A Voyage to the River Sierra-Leone, trader John Matthews noted that friends in this region had various expressions when greeting each other, including a process in which they would "shake hands, and snap the finger and thumb." Similarly, in the mid-1850s Missionary George Thompson observed different groups in Sierra Leone employing elaborate handshakes: "if long separated, they put their hands on each other's shoulders, draw them down each other's arms, and rub the hands together, always closing off with a very expressive snap of the finger."[67] In the mid nineteenth century there was an article publish in many American magazines entitled How DY'e Do. This article talked about Afrikans all around the world and how they gave dap. The article claimed that the fingers and joints were the most important components of the entire process: "seizing the hand, they pull away at the fingers until the joints begin to crack," listing variations among peoples living in both "lower" and "upper" Guinea.[68] Masai men in Africa greet one another by a subtle touch of palms of their hands (After spitting in them) for a very brief moment of time.[69] This is to fully endorse another member of the tribe or another tribe. 'In Liberia, the snap handshake or finger snap is a gesture of greeting, in which two people shake hands in the conventional Western way but end the handshake with a mutual press of the fingers that creates a "snap" sound.'[70] Every Afrikan in Amerika that

---

[67] Matthews, J. (1970). *A voyage to the river Sierra-Leone: With an additional letter on the subject of the African slave trade*. London: B. White.

[68] *The American freemason's new monthly magazine*. (1860). New York, NY.

[69] https://www.bidhaar.com/2020/08/03/the-spitting-of-the-maasai/

[70] Leanne Olson (2009). A Cruel Paradise: Journals of an International Relief Worker. Insomniac Press. pp. 50–. ISBN 978-1-897414-89-7.

grew up in the inner city of the United States of Amerika grew up doing both of the last two examples. The Afrikan influence on our social interaction is undeniable.

AAVE or Ebonics

When I was growing up mainstream Amerika started to call Afrikan Amerikan slang Ebonics. It was used simply to describe the spin we put on the English language and the colloquialisms we internalize and express daily. This term has now transitioned into AAVE standing for African American Vernacular English. AAVE is now defined as the variety of English natively spoken, particularly in urban communities, by most working and middle-class African Americans and some Black Canadians.[71] This expanded definition also comes with expanded analysis as now most linguist agree that AAVE is influenced by West Afrikan languages. They also note creole and pidgin as influences on AAVE.

Due to the trans-Atlantic slave trade, we spoke a variety of languages and learned them to survive. The evolution of this is also found amongst our Gullah Geechee family and Jamaican family found in their vernacular. My brothers Oriire and Kwaku Bekoe have done extensive research in this area.

---

[71] *Edwards, Walter (2004), "African American Vernacular English: Phonology", in Kortmann, Bernd (ed.),* A Handbook of Varieties of English: A Multimedia Reference Tool*, 2, Walter de Gruyter, pp. 366–382,* ISBN 9783110175325

The following chapters illustrate their point of similarities between AAVE and Afrikan languages.

1 The use of habitual tense markers

In this case we are using the term habitual tense marker to refer to words or phrases that indicate that someone does something routinely or consistently in other words habitually.

In Yorùbá language the habitual tense marker "máa ń" is used. For example if someone wanted to say "he usually fights" this would be translated as "*Ó (he/she) máa ń jà (to fight)*".

As someone who is accustomed to speaking AAVE the phrase "*he usually fights*" seems very odd.

The habitual markers typically used in AAVE are "*be*" and "*stay*".

The more natural way to say this phrase is "*He be fightin*" and if you wanted to add more emphasis "*He stay fightin*".

@oriire @kwaku.bekoe

2 Repetition of words to add emphasis

Let's look at a few examples of repetition in Twi:

"*Papaapa*" can be used to mean very good and is a replication of the word "*pa*" meaning good. "*Fɛfɛɛfɛ*" can be used to mean very beautiful and is the replication of the word "*fɛ*" meaning beautiful.

Repeating words to add emphasis is a very common practice in AAVE:

Let's look at a few examples:

"*Oh you grown grown*" > repeating the word *grown* emphasizes the fact that the person either is or thinks of themselves as very mature.

"*For real for real I'm ready to go*" > repeating the phrase *for real* emphasizes that the person is very serious about their statement.

"*I been been doing that*" > repeating the word *been* emphasizes the fact that the person has engaged in this action for a very long time and wants to make that clear to the listener.

@oriire @kwaku.bekoe

3 Elision and contraction in normal speech

In this case we are using the term elision to refer to the removal of one or more consonants from a word typically in fast speech.

Let's look at a few examples in Yorùbá langauge:
Òrìṣà > òòsà, Ènìyàn > èèyàn, Egúngún > eégún

Let's look at a few examples in AAVE as well:
I don't > I oun, I ain't > I ain, I don't even know > I oun een know

This is a longer and more complex topic but contractions are also very common in Yoruba language. In some cases two words are joined when the first word ends in a vowel and the second begins with a vowel i.e. "*lọ sí ọjà*" (go to the market) becomes "*lọ* sọ́jà".

Something similar happens in AAVE i.e. the words "*all of*" become "*alla*", the words "*bout to*" become "*bouta*" and "*going to*" becomes "*gonna*".

@oriire @kwaku.bekoe

These real-world examples along with the technical linguistic analysis really put in perspective how AAVE is connected to our Afrikan speech, language and thought. I truly would like to thank brother Oriire and Kwaku for their research in this matter, but I must also present more research from a sister named Djeneba Deby. Her work concerning multiple Afrikan languages illustrates the same point as brother Kwaku and Oriire. Allow me to present her findings.

Similarity between
Ebonics
Wolof
Esan and
Bamanankan

Twitter and IG: @farafinmuso

Emphasis:

- He a villain villain
- Obulu obulu

Expansion:

- From xam (to know in **Wolof**) to xam xam (science, knowledge)
- From bɛn (meaning agreement in **Bamanankan**) to bɛnbɛn (plot)

Repetitions also create rhythm and musicality in speech so this feature is very present in expressive adverbs. Repeating words also allow the speaker to convey the message that they want to get to the essence of the thing spoken about (you may have visited Philly, but you ain't seen Philly Philly).

In **Ebonics** in particular repetitions can shift the whole sense of what's being said.

Twitter and IG: @farafinmuso

Repetitions

In various African languages repetitions are used to add emphasis or to expand a term's concept.

Esan:

Yoyoyo (very reddish)

Obulu obulu (thank you very much)

Wolof:

Xam xam (science)

Dagg dagg (incision)

Bamanankan:

Bɛnbɛn (plot)

Yɛrɛ yɛrɛ (real)

Ebonics:

He a villain villain

For real for real

Twitter and IG: @farafinmuso

It is clear that our vernacular, slang, colloquialisms, and tongue expressions all have an Afrikan root.

Woke as The Ability to See

To be woke is the new cool in our society. People use phrases like "stay woke" "oh im not sleep I'm woke" to draw attention to the fact that they have some type of esoteric knowledge usually about history, politics, spirituality, or conspiracy. It's a part of our culture that have evolved from earlier forms of expression that mean the same thing. We used to say solid, speaking truth to power, kick knowledge, conscious and now woke. Woke basically mean you are aware to social injustice especially the ones effecting Afrikan people. To be woke one must be awake, that sounds silly to say but think about this in the literal sense. One's eyes must be opened to be woke. This is where our Afrikan spiritual traditions come into play. We did not just choose the word woke to describe what it describes by accident. In the Kongo they have a phrase called Bluwa Meso and it means to have one's eyes opened towards secrecy of life.[72] This is their version of woke, coming into knowledge to make them suitable to decode the mysteries of life. Not only does this open them spiritually but it gives them access to what is called Mbongi. Mbongi is the Kongo's political institution. So,

---

[72] Fu-Kiau, K. Kia Bunseki. (1985). *The mbongi : an African traditional political institution : a eureka to the African crisis.* Nyangwe, Zaïre: Omenana.

you make yourself fit to make decisions by becoming woke. Amongst the Wolof in Senegambia the griots (keepers of unwritten history) were also referred to as hepkat who a person is whose eyes have been opened and speaks the truth. Griots or Jele are held in high esteem by the entire community. So once again Knowledge is associated with being woke and also the respect from the community. Amongst the Igbo native doctors (dibia) were also entitled to wear chalk around either one or both eyes, depending on their seniority. The same was true of priests. Chalk around the eyes signifies an ability to see beyond the visible world and into the world of the spirits. Chalk is still used in this way among traditional doctors, diviners, and priests, as we have often encountered during our travels in Thomas's footsteps. They are sometimes called dibia anya nzu, meaning 'native doctor with the eye of chalk.'[73] Amongst the Ewe in Ghana who practice West Afrikan Vodun they warn against having these eyes opened if one is not ready.[74] Just like with any knowledge if one is not ready, they can go crazy or mad. Wokeness is something everyone is not ready for. Imagine how a devout Afrikan Muslim feels when he is told for the first time of

---

[73] Umeh, J. A. (1997). *After God is Dibia*. London: Karnak House.

[74] Sena Voncujovi Bokor (Priest of Fa)

the Islamic slave trade in Afrika that lasted nearly 1300 years. Opening those eyes to the truth is not advised for everyone. The Woke among us have opened their eyes to the truth spiritually and politically and are ready to take action, this hasn't changed from old Afrika to now.

Hoodoo

Hoodoo is something that came out of the remnants of Afrikan spiritual traditions. When we were enslaved in Amerika, we did not give up our right to practice our own traditions from home. We merely adapted them and sometime combined them to fit the current demographic wherever that was. According to Garvey F. Lundy etymologically scholars point out that Hoodoo is a phonetic approximation of the Ewe word *Hudu*, which is still used today. In West Africa, Hudu is a well-regarded religious tradition passed on through family priestly lines.

Hoodoo, in its most general sense, can be defined as a system of magic, divination, and herbalism widespread among the enslaved Africans in America. The goal of Hoodoo is to allow people access to supernatural forces to improve their daily lives in areas such as gambling, divination, cursing one's enemies or removing a curse, treatment of sickness, and many of the daily troubles of life. Some researchers, however, have attempted to distinguish the specialists within the broader field of conjure. They argue that conjurers can be divided into three categories: hoodooists, healers, and readers.[75] The ethnic groups brought to the

[75] Molefi Asante and Ama Azama Encyclopedia of African Religion

United States during the years of the slave trade were Kongo, Igbo, Akan, Mandé, Yorùbá, Fon, Ew e, and Fulbe, among many others.[76][77] After the arrival of diverse African ethnic groups to the United States, Hoodoo was created by enslaved African Americans for their spiritual survival as a form of resistance against slavery. "Because the African American community did not have the same medical or psychological aids as the European American society, its members were forced to rely on each other for survival." As a result, free and enslaved African Americans relied on Hoodoo for their protection. These powerful systems belonging to these many different ethnic groups from the Kongo, Nigeria, Ghana, Benin and various other West Afrikan place started to communicate and merge their spiritual practices for their survival. So, when you hear Bone Thugs and Harmony rap about seeing you at the crossroads don't be shocked, these types of things were passed down from generation to generation and although it may not be as frequent as once

---

[76]Ferguson. "Magic Bowls". *Park Ethnography Program*. Department of Interior - The National Park Service. Retrieved January 15, 2021.

[77] Cooksey, Susan (2013). "Kongo Across the Waters". *African Arts*. www.jstor.org: UCLA James S. Coleman African Studies Center. **46** (4): 79–82. doi:10.1162/AFAR_a_00109. JSTOR 43306192. S2CID 57565417. Retrieved January 15, 2021.

before it is still alive and well. Hoodoo cultures are so popular that it even made it into the movie Austin Powers. Austin Powers was known for his catch phrase “I think I’ve lost my mojo”. The box office hit had everyone saying this phrase, little did they know that the word and conception of mojo had an Afrikan root. Mojo is sometimes an amulet or prayer bag of various items that can help, heal, or hurt. There is a process to fixing a proper mojo. A ritual must be put in place in order to successfully prepare a mojo by being filled and awakened to life. This can be done by smoking incense and candles, or it may be breathed upon to bring it to life. Prayers may be said, and other methods may be used to accomplish this essential step. Once prepared, the mojo is "dressed" or "fed" with a liquid such as alcohol, perfume, water, or bodily fluids[78]. The bag becomes an entity onto itself, it is spiritual power and that’s what Austin powers was referencing whether he knew it or not. We Afrikans in Amerika already believe in Hoodoo; we just don’t recognize that we do. I know you’re probably reading this thinking you don’t well would you feed your hair to birds? Men are you cautious about eating a woman’s spaghetti? Older men would you be concerned if

---

[78] Alvarado, D. (2011). *The Voodoo Hoodoo Spellbook*. San Francisco: Weiser Books.

you found your underwear buried in the back yard? Have you ever wondered why when people get loud in the church, they call it shouting? All these are remnants of Hoodoo. Especially the shouting or as Hoodoist refer to it ring shouting. The term UDUNU (UDURU) meaning offering, the determinative symbol used is the which is a variation of the deben (teben) symbol... The term deben means circle, circuit, to make the circuit of or go around a place. With regard to ritual offering, those who practice Hoodoo in North Amerika as well as Akanfo in Ghana are familiar with our ritual dances during which spirit possession occurs, where the community and individuals who possess a spirit dance in a counterclockwise circle or circuit.[79] The ring shout in Black churches (African American churches) originates from African styles of dance. Counterclockwise circle dancing is practiced in West and Central Africa to invoke the spirits of the ancestors and for spirit possession. The ring shout and shouting looks similar to African spirit possession[80]. Most of us in the church have seen this and some of us have participated! Little did you know what you were actually doing until now.

[79] Weeksville heritage center

[80] Murphy, Joseph M. (1994). Working the Spirit: Ceremonies of the African Diaspora. Boston, Massachusetts: Beacon Press Books. pp. 145–175. ISBN 9780807012215.

Relation to the Black Church

People usually ask me about church and its effect on our emotions. Many of us experience double consciousness and cognitive dissonance when we find out the history of Christianity. We ponder to ourselves why we feel so good at church if the religion our family have been practicing for generations is based on someone else culture. Well, I believe the black church is special in this regard and it's designed to speak to our Afrikan heritage. In short no one does church like black people and many things we think is a product of the religion itself is actually things we instituted because of our familiarity with it. I'm talking about those mechanism that uplift us in service that are absent in non-black church's worship styles. Let's first start with the choir and you know what I mean by the choir. Black churches are famous for their choirs because of the rhythm and movement we possess. Marimba Ani calls this rhythm Ntu.[81] Ntu is the vital force in Bantu Ontology. In short, **Ntu** means a human being and it emphasizes that there is spirit of oneness and harmony among people and nature. The concept of **Ntu** emphasizes solidarity and oneness amongst Afrikan people in Ki.môyo.[82] Think about how the Ntu is found in church, we as

---

[81] Let the Circle Be UnBroken By Marimba Ani

[82] Asar Imhotep Personal conversation

a collective can't move to fast or to slow. We find this Ntu together and maintain this rhythm together.[83] Think about what we call the holy ghost in church, we say we caught the holy ghost, or we caught the sprit, is this not spirit possession? Is this not an Afrikan experience being defined by new world European terms? Can we argue that that as Marimba Ani puts it "The Church people have given an Afrikan interpretation to this European terminology?[84] I would say emphatically yes and its obvious to see these types of Afrikan influences in our black church when you study Afrikan Ki.môyo and visit non-black churches where this phenomenon is absent. Could this holy ghost have nothing to do with the Christian God and actually be our ancestral spirits trying to break through? That's a question for the Christians to ask themselves.

---

[83] Let the Circle Be UnBroken By Marimba Ani
[84] Let the Circle Be UnBroken By Marimba Ani

Music While Working

"We sang and moved until we were able to experience totally the spirit within us. We "got happy." It is this spirit that has not been altered by the European. It needed to be seen" and heard" and felt" every now and then, in order to be kept alive."[85] This quote by mama Marimba Ani speaks not only to a practice we used in slavery to pass time, but it also speaks to a spiritual connection to music that's innate to Afrikans and carried through generations by our culture. Mama Marimba goes on to say "Each of us gained the strength necessary to deal with our incarceration. Sometimes we prepared for rebellion."[86] This quote expresses that our music was and is multifaceted in purpose. There are songs or endurance, there are songs of love, songs of remembrance, and songs of war. Some of these songs birthed some of our best like Harriet Tubman and Demark Vesey. Afrikans that heard the songs of war and took up arms, Afrikans that heard the Akoben war horn sounding far away from its root in America. "Our music activates that Afrikan genetic memory bank and allows us to remember. "Our rituals, our songs, our music and dance became vehicles through which to contact the divine, media through which we reached the

[85] Let the Circle Be UnBroken By Marimba Ani
[86] Let the Circle Be UnBroken By Marimba Ani

spiritual source and so received sustenance and energy, from the knowledge of our specialness."[87] Mama Marimba speaks truth to power in this quote and some of what we use music for is backed by modern science today. Daniel Barolsky is a professor of music at Beloit College, and he states available evidence indicates that music favored by the listener can temporarily improve arousal or mood as well as elevate cognitive performance.[88] From this analysis we can deduce that Afrikan music did everything that mama Marimba told us it did during the slave trade and this music still has this effect today. My brother T'challa says it best "music is not just about the time and space that you're playing; it is also the time and space you're not playing. Participation requires full engagement of the mind and respect for one's space and time."[89]

---

[87] Let the Circle Be UnBroken By Marimba Ani

[88] https://www.businessnewsdaily.com/11294-music-effect-on-productivity.html

[89] Spears of the Mossi A Historical Survey of the Minds of African Warrior Scholars vol 1

Most Popular Afrikan Spiritual Practices (Ki.môyo)

We start this chapter with a tradition I practice and have been learning about actively for the last 3 years. That’s the tradition known by many things but amongst us traditional practitioners we call it Ìṣẹ̀ṣe Lagba Agbaye or Ìṣẹ̀ṣe. This word expresses what most people call Ifá. The reason why we don’t call the whole tradition Ifá anymore is because Ifá is the system of Orunmila and doesn’t encompass an entire tradition of Orisa practices from southwestern Nigeria. Each of these Orisa have their own practice, literature, songs, dances etc. The word Ìṣẹ̀ṣe is defined by Oloye (chief) Fama dictionary as primordial. Meaning beginning or in its earliest stages. It refers to the beginning of oneself and the beginning of the Yorùbá ethnic group as a people. The system of Ifá has an oracle and this oracle is full of verse, stories, poetry, songs etc. In the Odù Ifá: Ògúndá Ọ̀wọ́rín Ìṣẹ̀ṣe is related to one's biological Father, Mother, Orí (Destiny), and Ikin (Ifá). It is chanted as:

A dífá fún Ìṣẹ̀ṣe tíí ṣe olórí orò láyé

A bù fún Ìṣẹ̀ṣe tíí ṣe olórí orò ní ìwàrun

Bàbá ẹni

Ìṣẹ̀ṣe ẹni

Ìyá ẹni

Ìṣẹ̀ṣe ẹni

Orí ẹni

Ìṣẹ̀ṣe ẹni

Ikin ẹni

Ìṣẹ̀ṣe

Ìṣẹ̀ṣe ẹni

Ìṣẹ̀ṣe mọ̀mọ̀ làá bọ

Kí á tó bọ Òrìṣà

And translated as

Ifá divination was performed for Ìṣẹ̀ṣe

Our root and the leader of all rituals on earth

Also cast Ifá divination for Ìṣẹ̀ṣe

Our root and the leader of all rituals in heaven

One's father.

Is one's Ìṣẹ̀ṣe

One's mother.

Is one's Ìṣẹ̀ṣe

One's Orí

Is one's Ìṣẹ̀ṣe

One's Ikin

Is one's Ìṣẹ̀ṣe

It's the Ìṣẹ̀ṣe one would first sacrifice to

Before sacrificing to Òrìṣà[90]

Our beginnings are everything and we honor our beginnings with every breath we take, thought we make so we say Ìṣẹ̀ṣe L'agba Gbogbo Wa which means the tradition will stay with us always.

The Yorùbá people acknowledge a creator deity called Olódùmarè, he is known by other names, but Olódùmarè is the most common one. Olódùmarè is everything from the air we breathe to the Àṣẹ in our bodies. Olódùmarè is existence itself and out of this existence came other deities in the Yorùbá pantheon.

The pantheon I'm referring to are called respectfully Irunmole and Òrìṣà. These are the deities that humans appeal to for work to be done in their lives. They are often represented by aspects of nature, but some are not represented by nature at all, and their phenomenon is not represented in an observable fashion. Each Òrìṣà have towns in which they originate from, colors, literature,

---

[90] Adérẹ̀mí Ifákòleèpin Adérẹ̀mí
(Olúwo Ifáòleèpin) Founder and Chief Coordinating Officer
Society for the Ifá Practice in Nigeria (SIPIN)

festivals, modes of worship, taboos, favorite offerings, poetry and even days of worship. Each has its own epistemology and if we were to compare it to schooling today each would be a college level course. To learn the ways of just one of these Òrìṣà can take a lifetime and a half of studying. One nerve really stops learning and perfecting one's craft of Òrìṣà. One that wants to symbolically marry the Òrìṣà and be a caretaker of its mysteries require initiation. Although this is not required to be a worshipper it is the next step up from devotee and a step in the direction in becoming a priest of said Òrìṣà. After one completes training, they are recognized by their trainer as a priest and conduct ritual on their own and eventually train others. I will now name a few Òrìṣà of this pantheon so you can get a better understanding of them.

Ṣàngó: The King from Oyo. His colors vary but the most popular are red and white. He is a thunder, fire, rain and lighting deity. Hates liars and is a patron of justice. He speaks with fire and truth. He is a warrior and is known to have many wives and be fond of dancing. He is easily the most popular divinity in the diaspora.

Ọbàtálá: The magnanimous king that lives in Iranje, the blacksmith of heaven, the molder of children's heads, king of Òrìṣà, the one who multiples people. Most possibly the oldest Òrìṣà and most respected for his character and power. Many forms and names of this Òrìṣà exist and he is known for his white clothing.

Èṣù: The owner of the knotted club, Òrìṣà avenger, owner of 1400 gourds of medicine, the carrier of sacrifice to Olódùmarè, transcends of time and space. He is standing at the crossroads. A powerful divinity that is on both sides of the spectrum so to speak. So many aspects to this divinity but no matter how you feel about Esu, there is no getting around working with him. Colors are usually Red and Black

Ọ̀ṣun: River divinity of the Osun River and indigo dyer. Very quiet deity that bites. Known for elegance and beauty. Symbol for female empowerment.Very knowledgeable one that uses water to heal. She who washes brass before washing child, associated with fertility and wealth. Have one of the largest festivals annually in Osogbo Nigeria where she landed and made her home. Colors range from gold to yellow to green to even white.

Ọya: River divinity that is Sango's Favorite wife. A divinity that is more powerful than her husband. Known for commanding the wind spirits, transmutation into animals, fire, lightning, and also carries a sword. Loves to dance to Bata drums and beautify herself with camwood powder. Associated with Egungun masquerade.

Ògún: Ògún the owner of a coat of charms, the mad man with strong bones, He who controls the fire over the rains, The advocate for the orphan, he is a strong pillar of support for the honest, Ògún is like the pumpkin, he is difficult to slice, Ògún is like a powerful rainstorm, his water floods and his misfortune gets everywhere. The King of the forrest the deity of evolution and progression in society and the one that is known all over the world. The iron, the blacksmith, the hunter and the most feared deity of them all.

Also, in this pantheon are what we call Egúngún which are commonly referred to as Ancestors. Although in Nigeria referring to Egúngún as simply ancestors are not quite correct. Egúngún are like the deities of your lineage. In some cases, they guard your lineage and become just as much a part of your family as one's human family members. They are the families masquerade and come out during festivals with messages and power. Not every lineage has an Egúngún but those that do have a responsibility to bring their masquerade out and celebrate with them annually. They also must be worshiped. Your ancestors are more commonly referred to as the Yorùbá words alale or baba nla.

They can also be worshiped but in another way. Types of Egúngún vary from town to town and masquerades have names and distinctive dress.

AKOM

Let's now switch to the tradition in Ghana called Akom which is practiced by the Akan people. Akom is the general term given to a series of dances performed by the Akomfo. It is an intricate system of communication and healing that provides an opportunity for dancing to the specific cadences of religious drumming during what may be characterized as a spiritual gathering of the ancestors, the Abosom, and the people gathered who sing, clap, drum, and dance.[91] The Akomfo and Asofo are known as the priest of the tradition and the Abosom are like the Òrìṣà amongst the Yorùbá. The supreme being amongst the Akan is called Nyame and Nyame is the creator is referred to by using many titles like Onyankopong, or Odomankoma but as Ephiram Donkor tells us Nyame is life itself. He created the order in which things may be and exist therefore he or it is existence. The spiritual presence of Nyame is in all things, but just like Olódùmarè he is aloof and doesn't interfere in the dealings of man. Nyame created the Abossom which are lesser spirits the intervene on the behalf of man. The Akan say Nyamenimbirnyembir pa which mean Nyame's time is most ideal and this is because his time is a

---

[91] Molefi Asante and Ama Azama Encyclopedia of African Religion

surety, and they are one in the same.[92] For the Akan people immortality is achieved through a series of stages that include birth, ethical existence, and death on what they call wdaize or earth/world. Chronological age accompanied by altruistic endeavors that one can verify in the community is the path to immortality and becoming a Nsamanfo. The Nsamanfo dwell in a place called Samanadzie which is the abode of all qualified elders and is ruled by a primordial woman and mother of all living things named NaSaman.[93] Like most Ki.Môyo systems Akom has a patheon of deities. Let's go over a few here.

Akonnedi/Nana Akonnedi/Akonnedi Abena: is a female obosom whose bosomfie is located in the Larteh Kubease region of Ghana. She is regarded as the mother of all abosom, the head of the pantheon, and is said to mete out justice and give the final decision in difficult disputes.[94]

Nana Asuo Gyebi: is a wandering ancient river Abosom originally from the northern region of Ghana who resides in various places throughout the country, although he has made the Larteh Kubease region a special home. He also traveled as

---

[92] Imhotep Asar, Alauja Vol 2

[93] Ephirim-Donkor, Anthony African Personality and Spirituality The Role of Abosom and Human Essence

[94] Molefi Asante and Ama Azama Encyclopedia of African Religion

far as the United Sates to help the lost children of Africa reclaim their spiritual past. He is credited with bringing the Akan tradition to the United States because his priests were among the first to be initiated here. He is a male Abosom who is a protector and a great healer.[95]

Nana Adade Kofi: is a male warrior obosom of strength and perseverance and is from the Guan area of Ghana. He is said to be the youngest of Nana Akonnedi's children. He is the obosom associated with iron and metals, and his sword is often used to swear oaths of allegiance.[96]

Mmoetia: is a system of abosom who are most often recognized as "dwarfs" whose feet turn backward. They live throughout Ghana in the forests and are highly skilled in the use of herbs. Considered the great spiritual gatekeepers of the Akan tradition, they specialize in working with nature spirits for the purposes of healing.

Anansi: probably the most popular Abossom in the pantheon. Anansi is often depicted in popular tales interacting with the Supreme Being and other deities who frequently bestow him with temporary supernatural powers, such as the ability to bring rain or to have other duties performed for him.

---

[95] Molefi Asante and Ama Azama Encyclopedia of African Religion
[96] Molefi Asante and Ama Azama Encyclopedia of African Religion

Some folkloric traditions portray Anansi as the son of the Earth Mother Asase Yaa.[97] It is important to note, however, that Akan spirituality writ-large does not generally emphasize the worship of Anansi as an Abosom to the same extent that other established African trickster deities are worshiped in their respective religions; his connection to the sacred is ultimately believed to be irrelevant in comparison to his importance in Akan society, leading to an extensive debate on the subject.[98] Nonetheless, those who do recognize Anansi in a religious context in Akan spirituality acknowledge him as the Obosom of wisdom; he is even said to have created the first inanimate human body, according to the scholar Anthony Ephirim-Donkor.[99]

---

[97] Egerton Sykes; Alan Kendall (2001). Who's who in non-classical mythology. Routledge. p. 144. ISBN 978-0-415-26040-4. Retrieved 12 November 2019.

[98] Yankah, Kwesi.(1983) "The Akan Trickster Cycle: Myth or Folktale?" Indiana: African Studies Program, Indiana University. pg. 9-11 [2] Accessed on 3/16/19ISBN 0-941934-43-8

[99] Ephirim-Donkor, Anthony African Personality and Spirituality The Role of Abosom and Human Essence

WEST AFRIKAN VODUN

We will now discuss the tradition that has received the most negative propaganda thrown its way. That is the tradition of Vodun or Voodoo. We must first make the distinction that we will be talking about west Afrikan Vodun and not Haitian Voodoo. Most may thing these systems are the same or there is a direct line between them, but this simply isn't true. West Afrikan Vodun comes from present day Benin but was once called Dahomey. It's still a very big part of Benin's culture today and annual Vodun festivals attract many from all over the globe. Although present day Benin is Vodun birthplace you will find practitioners in Ghana, Togo and Nigeria among the Ewe, Aja and Fon people. The word Vodun means spirit in the Fon language and is the basis of the entire tradition. Working with spirits is Vodun. In view of this, the Fonnu (the Fon people) call Vodun by many names. Vodun is referred to as *Nubudo* (a principle that cannot be explicated, a force whose point of departure is not perceptible). Another name for Vodun is *Nugongon* (a concept whose meaning is deep). The Fon people also call Vodun by the name *Nujiwu* (a thrilling principle that must be revered, a spiritual force that is beyond anyone's genie). *Yèhwé* or *Vodun Yèhwé* (*Yè*: "silhouette, spirit"; and *hwé*: "sun, purity"; hence, pure spiri- tuality) is another name by which the Fonnu call Vodun. Finally, the Fon people call Vodun by yet another name, *Hun* ("blood, source of life").[100]

Priest of Vodun is called Hounan, Hunsi, Vodunsi, and Bokor amongst other names. They are the spiritual leaders in charge of leading rituals to achieve desired results. The divination system they use is called Fa in Benin and Afa in Ghana. It is directly derived from Ifá from the Yorùbá but there are cultural differences between all three. It is said amongst the AFA diviners that when the oracle is accessed that the question or problem goes all the way back to its source in Yorùbáland and returns with the answer. Like other Afrikan Ki.môyo the Vodun people believe in destiny. Destiny is a deity in itself called Se. Se is what you are supposed to be doing in life and was decided on before you reached earth in the spirit realm. There is an ewe proverb that says "to have beautiful children is because of your Se (destiny), to have a beautiful wife is because of your Se, to be intelligent is because of your Se, to be wealthy is because of your Se. Everything in your life is because of your Se"- Ewe proverb.[101] Se as a physical representation is molded out of clay and adorned with an Afrikan Grey parrot feather that is red in

---

[100] Molefi Asante and Ama Azama Encyclopedia of African Religion
[101] Sena Voncujovi ReVodution Afrikan Majick Temple

color. The Vodun practitioners call their ancestors Togbewo and Mamawo for female ancestors. Just like most Ki.môyo they are venerated, celebrated and worshipped. You probably have guessed by now that the Vodun have a pantheon of deities. Let's look at some of the major ones.

Nana Buluku: She gave birth to the two divine twins of Mawu and Lisa and is the queen mother goddess of the pantheon in some areas. I must note she is also an Orisa amongst the Yorùbá but has significantly less influence in Yorùbáland. It was she who prefabricated the universe, leaving to her two successors the task of its completion.[102]

Mawu Lisa: (also called *Segbo-Lisa*) are the creator couple of Heaven and Earth. Mawu, the female principle, corresponds to the moon and is associated with night, fertility, motherhood, gentleness, forgiveness, rest, and joy, all characteristics that one sees in women. Lisa, the male principle, corresponds to the sun and is associated with day, heat, work, power, war, strength, toughness, and intransigence, all things that characterize men.[103]

---

102 https://www.oxfordreference.com/view/10.1093/oi/authority.20110803100222778

103 Molefi Asante and Ama Azama Encyclopedia of African Religion

Sakpata: the oldest child of Mawu to whom the Earth was entrusted. He is the god of smallpox and the Vodun of wealth or prosperity. He is also known as Ayivodun (god of the Earth) or Ainon (proprietor of the Earth).

Heviosso or Hebiosso (also spelled Xêviosso or Xêbiosso) is also known as Jivodun: (Ji, sky; hence, Vodun of the sky): This is Mawu's second child, who is in charge of the sky, thunder, or lightning, and rain. He is the Vodun of Justice who punishes criminals and evil doers as well as anything, trees and animals, considered harmful, by striking them down, especially during rain. Xêviosso's cult is one of the most important cults in the western part of the Bight of Benin. This Vodun is represented by lightning rounds (or ammunitions) called sokpin and a thunder axe known as sossiovi.

Xu or Tovodun, also known as Agbé or Avlékété: the deity of the Ocean.

Gu or Ogu: the deity of iron. Gu is considered the Vodun of blacksmiths, warriors, and hunters. This Vodun does not condone evil doing insofar as he kills accomplices of wrong- doing when he is appealed to. A famous phrase among the Fon of Dahomey is "Yé da Gu do me" (to call on Gu to deal with someone or to send Gu onto somebody). Gu is represented by pieces of iron.

Aguê: the fifth child of Mawu, who is responsible for overseeing agriculture and the forests. This is the Vodun that reigns over birds and all animals.

Jo: the god of invisibility, the Vodun of the air.

Lègba: Mawu's youngest son, who barely received any endowments because all had been divided up among his older siblings. This accounts for his jealous inclination. He is, however, the guardian god considered as the town or country protector, but only on condition that offerings are regularly given to him.[104]

Tchamba: Slavery Deity that's known for punishing slave mastery and giving back what a lineage lost during slavery. This particular deity's shrine was brought to the USA by a continental Afrikan from Togo explaining how some families still have them in honor of the people in their family that was taken away in the slave trade. This practice was erased by colonialism.

---

[104] Molefi Asante and Ama Azama Encyclopedia of African Religion

HAITIAN VODU

We will now discuss the tradition known as Haitian Voodoo. Haitian Voodoo is famous because of the Hatian revolution in which Afrikan people from many walks of life and traditions unified to overthrow their oppressor and successfully becoming the first Afrikan independent nation. The Trans-Atlantic Slave trade brought many different Afrikans together on the island of Haiti. These Afrika people had a ceremony which is known in history as the Bois Caiman alligator spark ceremony. It's called this on the account of Bois Caiman means alligator forest and this is where the ritual took place. They called on the deities of their homelands and made a pact to destroy their enemy. Scholars in Haitian studies tend to agree that the years immediately following Haiti's slave revolution were crucial in shaping Haitian Vodou. African attitudes toward the land increased the retention of traditional religious practices. Unlike Cuban Santeria, which took shape primarily in urban contexts, Vodou emerged as a set of spiritual practices shaped largely by the ecological, social, and spiritual accommodations of peasant farmers. This history accounts for the importance of the land, sometimes literally of dirt or earth, in Haitian Vodou practices. A pinch of earth from a cemetery or a crossroads is a common ingredient in many kinds *of wanga,* a generic term for charms and talismans that are routinely used in Vodou *maji* (magic) and healing rites.

Cemeteries in rural Haiti are spiritual centers for the family. The graves of the oldest male and female buried in these cemeteries are spiritually empowered places, where members of the family can seek help from the ancestors and the Vodou spirits. Even some public cemeteries routinely function as churches or temples, places of communal Vodou ritualizing. This spiritual venue includes the dead in the ongoing ritual life of the extended Vodou family.

Important Vodou rituals are carried out *pye pa tè-a* (with feet on the earth). People who "serve the spirits" need to be connected to the earth. As a result of this alliance, the land itself becomes a text, open for interpretation. For example, the fertility of the land (or the lack thereof) is understood as a sign of the mood of the spirits and ancestors.[105]

Haitian Voodoo is often looked or described as simply West Afrikan Vodun in another place. This cannot be further from the truth. With careful study

---

[105] Philip Peek; Kwesi Yankah African Folklore: An Encyclopedia

one can see influences from the Kongo, Edo kingdom, Fon people, Yorùbá, and Akom practitioners and more. Brother Asar Imhotep has uncovered research that sheds light on the Kikongo influence in the Haitian revolution. He states "by the dawn of the Haitian Revolution. Blacks rallied against their white oppressors to the following battle-cry:

"He! He! Bonba! He! He!

"Kanga bafiote!

"Kanga, mundele!

"Kanga ndoki!

"Kanga li!

Meaning

"E! E! N'kisi M'bumba! E! E!

"Tie aIl blacks together (in the sense of unity)

"Tie aIl whites together (in the sense of annihilation)

"Tie up aIl traitors (whether black or white)

"Tie it up (the goal of liberation)[106]

Haitian Vodu have deities called Loa or Lwa. They separate pantheons of these Lwa by number. You will hear the term divisions or nanshons to separate these divinities. This number fluctuates but the range I have seen is 17-21. Think of these numbers as families of divinites. The most common families are the Rada (or Arada), the Kongo, the Ibo, the Petwo or Petro, and the Nago (or Anago). Simply the Rada are said to be derived of the old spirits from Afrika and the Petro were born in the violent revolution. Brother Leslie Desmangles breaks this phenomenon down further. The Wangol and Nago are the least known in Haiti and derive from the region of Angola. Ibo refers to Nigeria and Benin, whereas Rada derives from Arada, the name of an important kingdom in ancient Dahomey during the Haitian colonial period. Similarly, the Kongo lwas originated in the Bakongo region of West Africa, which was the place of origin of thousands of Africans sent to Saint Domingue. Petwo reportedly derives from a legendary character Dom Pedro, a leader of a rebellion during the latter half of the 18th century. Some lwas bear African-derived names such as Ezili Freda Dahomey and Damballah Wèdo, where both terms, Freda and

---

[106] Asar Imhotep No Specific Publication

Wèdo, derive from the name of the kingdom of Whydah in Dahomey. The lwas are said to reside in the mythological city of Vilokan in Dahomey or, more precisely, on a mythological island far below the sea that few privileged Haitians are said to have visited, having been taken there by the lwas.[107][108] Priest of Hatian Vodu is called Houngan and Mambo for the women. There are mentions of different types of divinations systems these priest use but the only name I have been able to uncover is Lèson. This is currently done with playing cards and. It is unclear if this is how it was traditionally done but there was another method that had to do with dreams and possibly possession. Dreams are vital sources of liturgical novelty in Haitian Vodou. Dreaming plays a key role as provocateur and shaper of this natality. Additionally, it serves as a vouchsafe for belief; as a transformative force; as a form of divination; and as a source for theological and liturgical information. Additionally, Vodou priests and priestesses utilize dreaming in their work with clients and it plays role in the enactment of spiritual marriages.[109] The Supreme deity of this system is called Bondye and it is Bondye that

[107] Desmangles, Leslie G. " Vodou." In Encyclopedia of Religious Rituals. New York: Routledge.
[108] Molefi Asante and Ama Azama Encyclopedia of African Religion
[109] McGee, A. M. (2012). Dreaming in Haitian Vodou: Vouchsafe, guide, and source of liturgical novelty. *Dreaming, 22*(2), 83–100. https://doi.org/10.1037/a0026691

maintain order throughout the universe but like deities that come from Afrika he is aloof and does not interact with man directly and has created lesser deities i.e Lwa to interact with man.[110] He is also called Olohoum or Olowoum which looks like it may have influence from the Yorùbá deity and words Olorun and Oluwo.[111] Within the Haitian Vodu pantheon there is a phenomenon called Veve. According to Milo Rigaud "The veves represent figures of the astral forces in the course of Vodoun ceremonies, the reproduction of the astral forces represented by the veves obliges the Loas to descend to earth. Every Loa has his or her own unique veve, although regional differences have led to different Veves for the same Loa in some cases. Sacrifices and offerings are usually placed upon them, with food and drink being most commonly used.[112]

Let's name some import Lwa/Loa within the Haitian Vodu pantheon.

---

[110] Fernández Olmos, Margarite; Paravisini-Gebert, Lizabeth (2011). *Creole Religions of the Caribbean: An Introduction from Vodou and Santería to Obeah and Espiritismo* (second ed.). New York and London: New York University Press.
[111] Thylefors, M. (2008). "Modernizing God" in Haitian Vodou? Reflections on Olowoum and Reafricanization in Haiti. *Anthropos*, *103*(1), 113–125. http://www.jstor.org/stable/40466868
[112] Rigaud Milo Secrets of Voodoo, City Lights, NY, 1969

Agassu: Dahomean in origin and belonging to the Fon and Yorùbá tribes. When a person is possessed by Agassu, his hands become crooked and stiffened, therefore resembling claws. In Dahomey, he is the result of a union between a panther and a woman. He is associated with water deities and sometimes takes the form of a crab. He is one of the mythical creatures who once gave assistance to the Ancestor.[113]

Damballah: Known as the serpent god, he is one of the most popular. Damballah is the father figure. He is benevolent, innocent, a loving father. He doesn't communicate well, as though his wisdom were too aloof for us. Damballah is the snake. He plunges into a basin of water which is built for him or climbs up into a tree. Being both snake and aquatic deity, he haunts rivers, springs, and marshes. Again, as the snake he is rather uncommunicative, but a loving quiet presence. Damballah does not communicate exact messages but seems to radiate a comforting presence which sort of sends a general spirit of optimism into all people present. Because of this, he is often sought after during ceremonies. When Damballah mounts someone the special offering to him is the egg,

---

113 https://sites.middlebury.edu/themoderncaribbean/files/2011/02/Haiti_-List-of-Loa1.pdf

which he crushes with his teeth. Damballah is the serpent god, also lightning. He and his wife, Aida-Wedo, are often shown as two snakes who look as if they were diving into the sink and by a rainbow. He is the bringer of rain; this is a necessity for good crops.[114]

Ezili Freda: Ezili's (also sometimes referred to as Erzulie) full name is Metrès (Mistress) Mambo Ezili Freda Dahomey. Each name refers to the different aspects of this Lwa of the Rada pantheon of Vodu in Haiti. She is by far the most popular female deity in Haiti, where she rules over love, romance, luxury, gambling luck, abundance, and refinement. Indeed, she is the symbol of love, femininity, and beauty. As a result of this close association of Ezili with womanhood, she is also perceived as the symbol of sexual fertility, the giver of children. It is to her that one appeals in conception and childbearing matters.[115]

The colors that symbolize Ezili are pink and white. Traditionally, she is served on Thursday because this is her sacred day. She is depicted as a rich woman, and to serve her, one must present the

---

114 https://sites.middlebury.edu/themoderncaribbean/files/2011/02/Haiti_-List-of-Loa1.pdf

115 Molefi Asante and Ama Azama Encyclopedia of African Religion

most expensive and elegant gifts in attempts to gain her affections and endowments.

Legba: Old man who guards the crossroads. He must be saluted each time a service or any other activity with the Loa will begin. Legba controls the crossing over from one world to the other. He is the contact between the worlds of spirit and of flesh. He can deliver messages of gods in human language and interpret their will. He is the god of destiny and is also the intermediary between human beings and divine gods,Legba is one of the most important Loa in Haitian voodoo. He is the first Loa to be called in a service, so that he can open the gates to the spirit world and let them communicate with other Loa. No Loa dares show itself without Legba's permission. Whoever has offended him finds himself unable to address his Loa and is deprived of their protection. He is the origin and the male prototype of voodoo. Voodooists believe that if Legba grants their wishes, they can contact the forces of the universe. He is the guardian of voodoo temples, courtyards, and crossroads. He protects the home. If you are going on a trip, it is believed that you pray to

Legba for protection from harm and a safe return home.[116]

Kalfu (Carrefour, Kalfou): Legba is twined with his Petro opposite. Kalfu too controls the crossroads. Actually, were it not for him the world would be more rational, a better place. Kalfu controls the evil forces of the spirit world. He allows the crossing of bad luck, deliberate destruction, misfortune, injustice. Kalfu controls the in-between points of the crossroads, the off-center points. Legba controls the positive spirits of the day. Kalfu controls the malevolent spirits of the night. Yet Kalfu can control these evil spirits too. He is strong and tall, muscular. People do not speak in his presence. He claims that most of the important Loa know him, and he collaborates with them. He is the grand master of charms and sorceries and is closely associated with magic.[117]

Let's discuss the spiritual system of Palo Mayombe also known as Las Reglas de Congo. Palo comes out of Cuba with influence of the Kongo via the trans-atlantic slave trade. Palo the

---

116 https://sites.middlebury.edu/themoderncaribbean/files/2011/02/Haiti_-List-of-Loa1.pdf

117 https://sites.middlebury.edu/themoderncaribbean/files/2011/02/Haiti_-List-of-Loa1.pdf

word means stick and sticks are very important for they are used to make powerful medicine called Nganga also known as Prenda and another form of medicine called Nkisi. The Nganga may refer to a spirit n'kisi or to a clay container, gourd, sack or the iron cauldron that contains the spirit.[118] Palo Mayombe is based of the Kongolese spiritual traditions of Lemba, Kimpasi and Kinkimba. Dr. Fukiau denotes that cultural influences have transformed this practice into what is known as Palo Mayombe today. Palo is associated with sending spirits out for missions and using the dead as powerful spiritual forces for protection, or attack. The spirit in the Nganga is generally refered to as the slave of the Palero and the activities he is directed to do is called trabajos.[119] Practitioners of these traditions are called Paleros. Palo teaches that the individual comprises both a physical body and a spirit termed the sombra ("shade"). In Palo belief, these are connected via a cordón de plata ("silver cord"). In Cuba, the Bakongo notion of the spirit "shadow" has merged with the Spiritist notion of the perisperm, a spirit-vapor surrounding the human body. The dead, referred to as the Egun, play a prominent role in Palo. It is held that

---

[118] Molefi Asante and Ama Azama Encyclopedia of African Religion
[119] Palmié, Stephan (2013). "Signal and Noise: Digging up the Dead in Archaeology and Afro-Cuban Palo Monte". Archaeological Review from Cambridge. **28** (1): 115–131.

ancestors can contact and assist the living, with paleros/paleras venerating the souls of their ancestors.[120] Priest of these traditions are called Tata and they make Nganga for initiates. The divination system for this tradition is called Ndungui,[121] which entails divining with pieces of coconut shell, and the chamalongos, which uses shells. The supreme deity in this tradition is called Nsambi, this is the same name for the traditions of the Kongo in which Palo is derived from with a slightly different spelling. In the Kongo the s is replaced with a z. Like mist Afrikan traditions Palo has a pantheon so let's name some of the Kimpungulu/ Mpungu.

Lucero Mundo: is the Custodian, messenger and spokesman for the Palo Mayombe temples, he is in charge of directing the steps to the consecration of the person who is going to initiate, because it is the first thing you get to give the necessary stability to the person. Without Lucero there is nothing in Palo Mayombe, is the first to receive the offerings and

---

[120] Fernández Olmos, Margarite; Paravisini-Gebert, Lizabeth (2011). Creole Religions of the Caribbean: An Introduction from Vodou and Santería to Obeah and Espiritismo (second ed.). New York and London: New York University Press.

[121] Fernández Olmos, Margarite; Paravisini-Gebert, Lizabeth (2011). Creole Religions of the Caribbean: An Introduction from Vodou and Santería to Obeah and Espiritismo (second ed.). New York and London: New York University Press.

is first which must be addressed. The archetype of this divinity is related to children. Lucero Mundo is a standalone spirit in its existence and operation, and sometimes difficult to understand his character, that sometimes gets a little violent, which is why you should speak with humility and respect and conscious is commanded to execute the request, so you're always next to each other. Lucero Mundo is the beginning and the end, alpha and omega, life and death, hence its primary colors: red, representing the blood (life) and the black represents darkness (death).

Sarabanda: is the mpungu of war, iron, conflicts, protection, bloodshed, vengeance, and darkness. He is temperamental, fierce, powerful and protective, can remove serious obstacles, challenges and negative situations, yet he can be very giving at times. All of his offerings should be taken to the railroad tracks. He favors plantains, rum, cigars, machetes and the colors of green, black and coral. His wisdom, strength, and fierceness are unmatched and truly irrefutable. He is commonly referred to as being the strongest spirit and has no issue with such a title. He accepts Watariamba's children as his own and defends his children with such extreme ferocity that in most cases even the most wicked and highest of priests want nothing to do with wishing harm upon his children.

Mama Chola: is the Mpungu of love, and her seductive and sensual power encapsulates the feminine ideal. In nature, she rules over rivers. Her colors are yellow and gold, her number is 5 (and multiples of 5). Her day of the week is Saturday.

She exhibits all of the characteristics associated with fresh flowing water: she's lively, sparking, vivacious, refreshing. No one can resist her seductive laugh, her graceful dancing, and her lips that taste like honey. She has a lush womanly figure with full hips, which suggest eroticism and fertility. She loves silks, perfumes, fans and mirrors, all kinds of jewelry, she wears golden bracelets that jingle seductively when she moves, and her favorite treat is honey.

Tiembla Tierra: is an old man that is nicknamed "Father Time" because his existence goes as far back as the creation of earth and is said to be the father of all the other mpungo. He is the mpungo of mountains, mystics, and fathers. A wise and kind being, he can also be a fierce warrior. He is synonymous with purity, clear thinking and staying calm in extreme conditions. He favors all things white. Coconuts, unsalted rice, cocoa butter, parrot feathers, cool clear water and a wooden staff are among his favorite things. His offerings should be taken to a mountain. He represents coolness of thought, wisdom and clarity. Snails, white elephants and rainbows are associated with him also.

KMT

Let's now discuss the most popular Ki.môyo in the USA and the in the spiritual system that has no official name but comes from modern day Egypt classically known as KMT or Kemet. Contrary to popular belief the spiritual system of classical Egypt is not vastly different than the systems we see in inner Afrika. One key difference is Kmt and their history is so well documented that we get to see it evolve through dynastic periods, rulership, conflict and eventual collapse. Kmt has had multiple creator deities that have served as head of the pantheon at one time. There were also lesser dieites called Ntchr or Ntchrw in which served as intermediaries between the creator deity and man. The people of KMT believed in the Afterlife and that everyone had the chance to experience life in the duat(underworld). I say the change because there was a test one must pass to pass into this duat. On the scales of Ma'at one must place their heart and if it is lighter than a feather one can enter but of not a beast named Ammit would devour this person. The people of KMT believed in ancestor veneration hence we see the world-famous mummies and canopic jars. The Canopic jars were a part of the mumification process in which the stomach, intestines, lungs, and liver were placed, this is because all of which was believed would be needed in the afterlife. These organs were removed from the body and carefully treated with natron (a natural preservative used by embalmers) and placed in the sacred Canopic Jars.[122] Many Old Kingdom canopic jars were found empty and damaged, even in undisturbed tombs. Therefore, it seems that they were never used as containers. Instead, it seems that they were part of burial rituals and were placed after these rituals, empty.[123] These jars were decorated with the sacred writing of the people which is called the mdw ntchr which is translated to divine words. Often, they were made in the image of the Ntchrw Hapi, Duamutef, Imsety, Qebehsenuef. (Pictured below). These Ntchrw represented the 4 cardinal points and were a symbol of deities of these directions that provided protect on one's journey to the afterlife. They were also sons of a principal deity in kmt by the name of Heru. Heru is the divine child of Asar and Aset. The four sons of Heru are deities who act as pathfinders at the ascension of the dead and are responsible for protecting the body of the

---

[122] Strudwick, Helen (2006). The Encyclopedia of Ancient Egypt. New York: Sterling Publishing Co., Inc. pp. 184–185. ISBN 978-1-4351-4654-9.

[123] Lucie Jirásková: Damage and repairs of the Old Kingdom canopic jars – the case at Abusir. In: Prague Egyptological Studies. 15, 2015, ISSN 1214-3189, pp. 76–85, (online).

deceased, particularly the internal organs, from hunger and thirst.[124] For example, Hapi is one of the four sons of Horus (Heru). The sons of Heru are seen frequently in the Canopic jars used during mummification. In this context, the jar of Hapi has the head of a baboon and is said to be the guardian of the lungs.[125] Early canopic jars were placed inside a canopic chest and buried in tombs together with the sarcophagus of the dead.[126] In later periods they were placed in the four corners of the temple.[127] Next, the priests began the process of salting the body by placing it in natron for about 35 days. The priests often used henna or ochre to dye the limbs of the corpse after the application of the natron. Thus, the male corpse appeared red and the female corpse yellow after this process. One can see this pattern reflected in some of the paintings on the walls of the temples and tombs. They would then pack the chest and abdomen with pieces of material provided by the family of the dead person. Relatives might bring their special

---

[124] Molefi Asante and Ama Azama Encyclopedia of African Religion
[125] Molefi Asante and Ama Azama Encyclopedia of African Religion
[126] Budge, Sir Edward Wallis (2010) [1925]. The mummy; a handbook of Egyptian funerary archaeology. New York: Cambridge University Press. ISBN 978-1-108-01825-8.

[127] Budge, Sir Edward Wallis (2010) [1925]. The mummy; a handbook of Egyptian funerary archaeology. New York: Cambridge University Press. ISBN 978-1-108-01825-8.

fabrics to be placed inside the corpse for the journey to eternity. It was important that the priests soak the wads of material in various gums, herbs, and unguents so that the body could be molded and shaped to its original form. Then the opening in the left side of the cadaver was covered with a plaque that was protected by the Four Sons of Heru.[128]

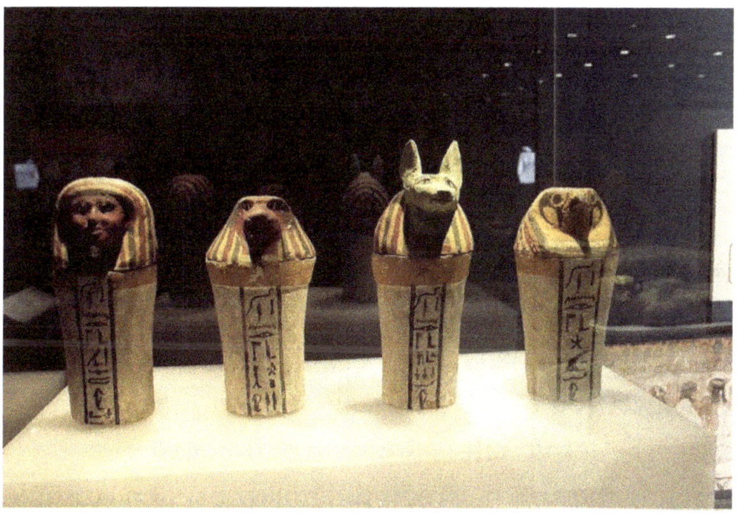

The pantheon of KMT had many deities but we can only focus on a few of them. Priest of the traditions of Kmt had many names but the most basic name I have found for priest is wnwt. A priest of the Ntchr Amen was called
ḥm nṯr tpj n jmn and the Priest of Ra were called wr-mꜣw which translates to great seer.

[128] Molefi Asante and Ama Azama Encyclopedia of African Religion

Ptah: A creator deity who is over craftsmen and design. Ptah is one of the oldest deities in the pantheon and is usually depicted with his WAS scepter representing power. Ptah is from what is known as Menefer and is credited with bringing the world into being with the power of speech. A hymn to Ptah dating to the Twenty-second Dynasty of Egypt says Ptah "crafted the world in the design of his heart," and the Shabaka Stone, from the Twenty-Fifth Dynasty, says Ptah "gave life to all the gods and their *ka*s as well, through this heart and this tongue.[129]

Ra: A creator deity represented by the Sun. He is from Iwnw or what's most commonly known as Heliopolis. Ra has many forms due to the many manifestation of the sun at different times. You have Khepra which is the rising sun, Ra Horakthy which is the sun between the horizons, and Atum the setting sun. Although these are different ntchrw with their different depictions and statues they are all still Ra. This is one of the reasons why Ra is regarded as one if not the most important ntchr in the entire patheon.

---

[129] Allen, James P. (1988). Genesis in Egypt: The Philosophy of Ancient Egyptian Creation Accounts. Yale Egyptological Study. pp. 38–41

Asar: Asar or Wsir or more commonly known as Osiris is the father of Heru and husband of Aset. He is one of the first kings of the pantheon and therefore he is frequently depicted with the royal crook and fail. He is associated with vegetation, afterlife, and agriculture. After being dismembered into eight pieces by his rival Set, Asar was resurrected by his wife and became the lord of the underworld. Through the hope of new life after death, Asar began to be associated with the cycles observed in nature, in particular vegetation and the annual flooding of the Nile, through his links with the heliacal rising of Orion and Sirius known as Sabu Septa at the start of the new year.[130]

Heru: Heru is the divine child of Asar and Aset whose importance came to be represented in kingship in Kmt. He is represented by a falcon archetype and is one of the guardians of KMT. He is most famous for his battles with Set in the Asarian myths. In these battles he loses an eye, and this eye becomes the famous eye of Heru. The symbol of the Eye of Horus that is, wedjat was used for protection, healing, as well as mathematical and medicinal calculations in ancient

---

[130] The Oxford Guide: Essential Guide to Egyptian Mythology, Edited by Donald B. Redford, pp. 302–307, Berkley, 2003, ISBN 0-425-19096-X

Egypt. In fact, the Eye of Horus, or all- seeing eye, is one of the most recognized symbols of ancient Egypt. It was in use throughout the thousands of years of Egyptian civilization and continues to be used today.[131]

[131] Molefi Asante and Ama Azama Encyclopedia of African Religion

Less Popular Afrikan Spiritual Practices (Ki.môyo)

We will now discuss the lesser known Afrikan spiritual practices from inner Afrika. We will start with the system that comes from my father's land with is Senegambia. This tradition is called A Fat Roog which translates to way of Roog. Roog or Koox is the creator deity at the head of the pantheon that is responsible for all of creation. According to the Seerer Resource Cernter he shares attributes and common origin with African deities such as Fa Ro or Faro (Bambara), Wa Roongo or Warongwe (Sandawi), Ruanga (Nyoro), and Ra (Ancient Egyptian).[132] The creation of Planet Earth was a result of a swamp which the first tree grew within. The first three worlds created through a mythical egg and under the principles of chaos were: the waters of the underworld, the air including the higher world and earth. These three were the first primordial worlds created by the supreme being through thought, speech, and action. Planet Earth was not created until long after the creation of these worlds. The contentious points are which of the main sacred

---

[132] Seerer Resource Center Private email

trees in Serer society (below) grew not just first, but also within the primordial swamp on earth.[133]

The sacred Trees are as follows:

- Saas (var: Sas) - Acacia albida
- Nquf (var: Ngudor NGuf- Guiera senegalensis. Somb - Prosopis africanaa species of Prosopis
- Nqual (var: Ngaul or NGawal- Mitragyna inermis part of Rubiaceae family of the genus Mitragyna
- Mbos - Gardenia ternifolia[134]

These Trees were the first living things on earth and were intrically apart of the formation of earth. This system belongs to the Seereer people and is still practiced today. Their priest of this tradition is called Saltigue is pronounced "Sal-ti-gi" and sometimes spelled Saltigi, they once called Lamans but over time the name changed. The Saltigue priest were responsible for assisting the king with the prosperity of the country. In this role,

---

[133] Tamsier Joof (founder of the SRC)

[134] (in French) Lericollais, André, « La gestion du paysage ? Sahélisation, surexploitation et délaissement des terroirs sereer au Sénégal », Afrique de l'ouest, Dakar (21–26 November 1988), ORSTOM, [3] For the name of Serer medicinal plants and their corresponding Latin names, see: *Nqaul* is spelt *Ngaul* (p. 8), *Mbos* (pp. 5 & 8), *Somb* (p. 8), *Ngud* (p. 8), *Nalafun* (p. 8), *Ngol* (p. 8), *Saas* is spelt *Sas* (p. 5), and [4] (Retrieved 3 June 2012)

they were responsible for predicting the future of kings; the weather to come (for the purposes of agriculture); any natural disaster or political catastrophe that could befall the country; etc. As such, they were frequently consulted by the Serer kings (Maad a Sinig and Maad Saloum) preferably at the beginning of the rainy season.[135] There were also Griots in this society and system. Griots were the story tellers, musicians, genealogists, and truth tellers of the society. The Seereer people used to bury some griots in baobab trees, but they no longer do this. The baobab is sacred for various reasons: it is used for food and for medicinal purposes. It is also the dwelling place of some Pangool and is highly revered. Contrary to some scholars (usually Western scholars who do not understand the culture) who claim that the Seereer did not value the griots hence why they were buried in baobab trees, that is further from the truth. The baobab is revered as one of the most sacred trees in Seereer society. If griots were worthless, they would not have been buried there. Further, the griots were regarded as extremely special and powerful, with links to the supernatural world as well as guardians of knowledge and

---

[135] Sarr, Alioune, *Histoire du Sine-Saloum*, Introduction, bibliographie et notes par Charles Becker, BIFAN, Tome 46, Serie B, n° 3–4, 1986–1987. p31

history. Our Seereer ancestors believed that if a griot was buried in a graveyard like other common people, rain would not come hence why they were deposited inside one of the most sacred trees in Seereer society (the baobab, sometimes accompanied by grave goods). Further, our Seereer ancestors used to use big trees (usually the baobab tree) to mark dates or the passing of events or winter months. The number of markings symbolizes a person's age or the number of years that have passed since an important historic event. Since huge trees of this nature last for centuries, the history of a family or the society were documented on those trees along with the use of the Raampa script. The baobab tree is a tree of history and as guardians of history, our Seereer ancestors saw it fitting to bury the most revered griots inside a baobab. Just because one was a member of the griot caste did not mean one deserved a baobab burial. Only the most revered griots were buried in a baobab. Other common griots were buried in a grave just like anybody else. Nothing special about them. Kings, queens, and important figures were mummified and buried in tomb just like they used to do in Ancient Egypt, and always accompanied by grave goods to the afterlife. Professor Cheikh Anta Diop, Louis Diène Faye, Marguerite Dupire, Issa Laye Thiaw, and several other scholars have written a lot about the old Seereer mummification and burial system.[136]

Kings are called Maad and you will frequently see the area they ruled after the word for king. For example, if the king ruled sinig or saluum you would see Maad a Sinig or Maad a Saluum. Jaraff pronounced "Ja-raf." The Jaraff was the head of the Seereer noble council of electors responsible for electing the kings from the royal bloodline. If a Seereer king dies without nominating his heir (buumi),. the Jaraff could step in as king regnant until a suitable candidate can be found from the royal line. The Jaraff was therefore the most important person after the king.[137] There are also a hierarchy of kings amongst this system. Maad is sometimes spelled Ma'at (yes like the Egyptian word) but one can only be a Ma'at if the king has supernatural powers to intercede with the Divine and the cosmos in order to bring rain or change the climate, etc. That title was reserved for the ancient Seereer Lamans who landowners and kings by divine right were and were also expected to bring rain and abundance. Hence why they were ritually killed if they could not fulfill that function. For a Seereer king to be referred to as Maat, he must be of royal blood and has supernatural powers

[136] Seerer Resource Center Private email
[137] Seerer Resource Center Private email

endowed upon him by the Supreme Being (Roog).[138] One of the most important cosmological stars of the Serer people is called Yoonir. The "Star of Yoonir" is part of the Serer cosmos. It is very important and sacred and just one of many religious symbols in Serer religion and cosmology. It is the brightest star in the night sky, Sirius B. With an ancient heritage of farming, "Yoonir" is very important and sacred in Serer religion, because it announces the beginning of flooding and enables Serer farmers to start planting seeds.[139] Yoonir, symbol of the Universe, a Star with five points, outlined diagonals: Pentagram. The peak of the Star (top point) represents the Supreme Deity (Roog). The other four points represent the cardinal points of the Universe. The crossing of the lines ("bottom left" and "top right" and "top left and bottom right") pinpoints the axis of the Universe, that all energies pass. The top point is "the point of departure and conclusion, the origin and the end." Among the Serers who cannot read or write the Latin alphabet, it is very common for them to sign official documents with the Star of Yoonir, as the Star also represents "good fortune and destiny."[140] There are Family Totems called Taana in this tradition as well that are connected to

---

[138] Seerer Resource Center Private email

[139] Gravrand, "Pangool", pp. 21 and 468

[140] Gravrand, "Pangool", pp. 21 and 468

sacred animals. One cannot harm or eat the animal of their totem.

The following are family Totems (Taana) in A Fat Roog

- Joof Family Antelope
- Njaay or Njie Family Lion
- Sene Family Hare
- Saar Family Giraffe and Camel[141]

The intermediary deities of this culture are called Fangool (singular) or Pangool (plural).

Fangool – the singular of Pangool

Pangool – a group of Fangool

O Yaal Pangool (var: yaal pangool) – the masters of the Pangool cult, i.e. the Serer priestly class – Saltigues, previously the Lamanic class.

Pangool ke – the ancestors

The etymology of fangool comes from the Serer phrase Fang Qool which means the sacred serpent the plural of which is pangool. Fangool means serpent.[142]

---

[141] Jean-Marc Gastellu (M. Sambe – 1937 [in]), *L'égalitarisme économique des Serer du Sénégal*, IRD Editions (1981), p. 130, ISBN 2-7099-0591-4.
[142] Gravrand, "Pangool", p 313

There are two main types of Pangool: non-human Pangool and human Pangool. Both are sacred and ancient, but the former is more ancient as a general rule. The non-human Pangool includes ancient sacred places with vital spiritual energies and personalized as such. These Pangool generally are the personifications of natural forces. Human Pangool, on the other hand, became Pangool once they are canonized after death. Thus, some are ancient, others are medieval. Through their intercession with the divine, they form a link that transmits vital energies. Not every dead ancient ancestor is canonized as Pangool.[143]

Pangool can be subdivided further into:

- **Pangool** who are known and revered in a particular region, such as the tombs of ancient Serer kings and queens (see Serer ancient history and Serer creation myth)
- **Pangool** who are known and revered in a particular village or town, such as the Serer village or town founders.
- **Pangool** who are known, revered, and venerated in a particular square such as the founder of the square.

---

[143] Gravrand, "Pangool", p 313

- a Fangool made known to an individual and thus became the personal Fangool of the individual in question, such as the Fangool Ginaaru (the personal Fangool of Maad a Sing Maysa Wali Jaxateh Manneh, var: Maysa Waaly Dione, the first Guelowar king of Sine, reigned: 1350–1370.
- those Pangool whose names are lost to history or did not disclose their identity, but are well known for certain events in Serer history, such as the seizure of certain historical figures, etc.
- In addition to these, Pangool can be further categorized depending on their character and nature, such as:

- Blood or red Pangool: those who require the sacrifice of domesticated animals (i.e.,cattle) in their veneration, or alcohol
- Milk Pangool: those who require the offerings of milk.
- Water Pangool': those who reside in water, etc.,
- Blood is a sign of life in Serer cosmogony and these types of Pangool fulfill a vital role in Serer society and are seen as one of the most ancient and powerful. The Fangool Ngolum Joof (var: Ngolum Diouf) is one of these blood Pangool. In many cases, offerings of alcohol rather than the sacrifice

of domesticated animals are made to these blood Pangool. In contrast to the blood Pangool, the milk Pangool such as Moussa Sarr, Njemeh (var: Ndiémé) of Languème and Njoxona, etc., are those Pangool who are peaceful in nature and character. They even reject anything that symbolizes violence or things that may evoke destruction or death, i.e., iron, weapons, gunpowder, blood and the color red. They usually are the protectors of Serer cities and the defenders of the weak[144].

Below is the symbol of the Seereer Resource Center but it also gives you a great visual to what the symbol of the Fangool looks like.

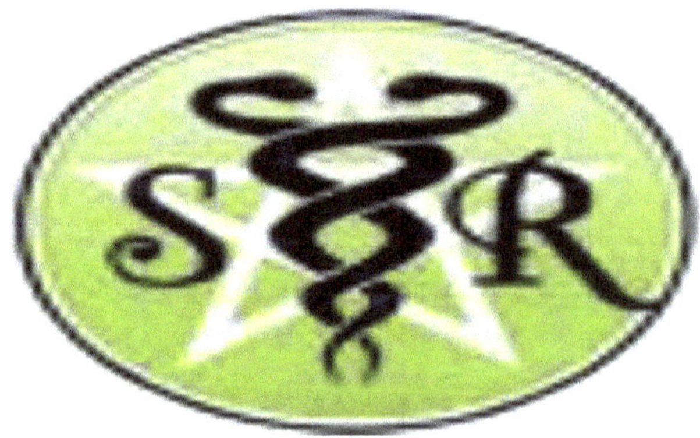

[144] Seereer Resource Center

EKPE The Leopard Society

Ekpe is an ancient Afrikan wisdom center that incorporating art forms and performance styles of dance, music, and esoteric knowledge of its tribe. Its origins remain obscure over centuries of its existence, but it is nonetheless acknowledged to be an invention of communities inhabiting the forest region of West and Central Africa. Ekpe`, in its literal translation, means 'the leopard', an animal conceived by traditional Africans throughout the forest belt to be a symbol of strength, tenacity, agility and vitality. These virtues were considered necessary for any well-organized society that aspired to order, peace and stability. But why the leopard of all animals? Used as a symbol of royalty and leadership in many parts of Africa, within the Cross River region the leopard has become the personification of the Ekpe` society itself. Generally, within African perceptions of the mysterious, the leopard is a 'sacred' animal that is active in the night when ordinary humans are dormant. The reverence accorded to the leopard seems justifiable to the native since it is corroborated by the fact that this animal is at the top of the food chain, devouring all others while remaining secure, stable and unsubdued.[145] Ekpe

[145] https://www.afrocubaweb.com/ivormiller/Miller-Ojong2012-s.pdf

had its origins in the non-Igbo Ekoi (or Ejagham) club, located east of the Cross River and named after the leopard, whose emblem is the repeated triangular pattern called agu, meaning “leopard’s paw.” Uli designs from Arochukwu include variations of repeated triangles (agu), checkerboard patterns, and four-sided shapes, and these motifs and their arrangements resemble the patterns that are found in the distinctive indigo blue and white ukara cloth worn by male members of the Ekpe society.[146] The cloth is made of plain cotton but transformed into a ritual object when nsibidi symbols are inscribed onto it through indigo dyeing. Nsibidi is a body of ideographic, abstract, and gestural signs deployed by the Ekpe society as a form of coded communication. In part because of their appropriation, exclusive use, and understanding of nsibidi, Ekpe members in the pre-colonial past were thought to have access to the spiritual realm and were, therefore, empowered to make and enforce societal rules and norms. While their political authority is largely diminished today, Ekpe membership is still prestigious and the society continues to be a unifying force among the

---

[146] Willis, E.A. 1997. Uli Painting and Identity: Twentieth-Century Developments in the Art of the Igbo-Speaking Region of Nigeria. Ph.D. thesis. University of London.

Ejagham, Igbo, Efik, Ibibio, and other cultural groups in the Cross River region.[147]

Worn as personal wrappers during initiations and at social events, ukara cloth distinguishes Ekpe members. Covering, concealing, and protecting their bodies, it functions as a physical metaphor for the ideological secrecy that the Ekpe society carefully constructs and guards. Ukara cloth also consecrates the interior of Ekpe lodges, where larger versions of the cloth hang as backdrops. Imbued with transcendental aura, ukara conveys the sacrality and prestige of the Ekpe secret society.

The Igbo 'Ukara' cloth of the Ekpe society, covered in Nsibidi is used to design the 'ukara ekpe' woven material which is usually dyed blue (but also green and red) and is covered in nsibidi symbols and motifs. Ukara ekpe cloths are woven in Abakaliki, and then they are designed by male nsibidi artists in the Igbo-speaking towns of Abiriba, Arochukwu and Ohafia to be worn by members of the Ekpe society. Symbols including lovers, metal rods, trees, feathers, hands in friendship war and work, masks, moons, and stars are dyed onto ukara cloths. The cloth is dyed by post-menopausal

[147] African Folklore: An Encyclopedia edited by Philip M. Peek, Kwesi Yankah

women in secret, and young males in public. Ukara was a symbol of wealth and power only handled by titled men and post-menopausal women. Ukara can be worn as a wrapper (a piece of clothing) on formal occasions, and larger version are hung in society meeting houses and on formal occasions. Ukara motifs are designed in white and are placed on grids set against an indigo background. Some of the designs include abstract symbols representing the Ekpe society such as repeating triangles representing the leopard's claws and therefore Ekpe's power. Ukara includes naturalistic designs representing objects such as gongs, feathers and manilla currency, a symbol of wealth. Powerful animals are included, specifically the leopard and crocodile.[148] The Ukara cloth is what was betrayed in exaggerated fashion amongst the border tribe in the movie Black Panther.

[148] African Folklore: An Encyclopedia edited by Philip M. Peek, Kwesi Yankah

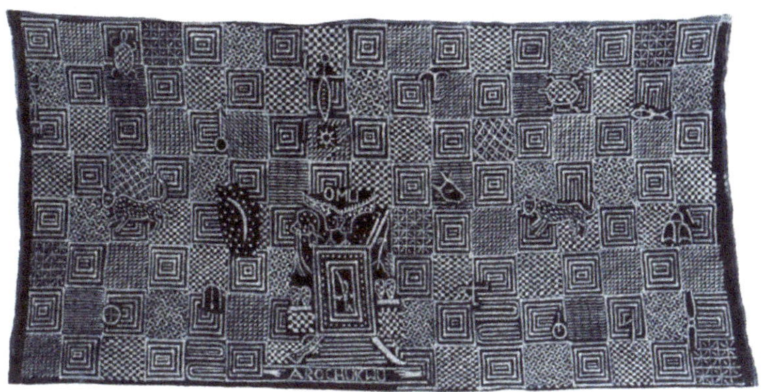

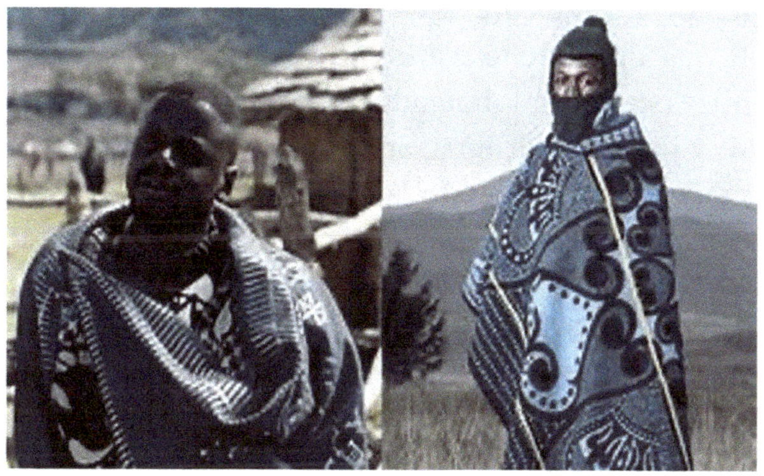

Akwa Ibom people used traditional cultural institutions such as Ekpo and Ekpe to maintain order in the society. These institutions stood out as government of the time. Ekpo is founded on the belief in life after death and is regarded as the soul or ghosts of ancestors that return to the land of the living in masquerade form to participate with their kinsmen in communal festivals such as farming and rite of passage. In Akwa Ibom, we have may masquerades like **Ekpo**, **Ekpe**, **Utuekpe**, **Ekpri Akata**, **Atat**, **Obon**, **Ntok Odio-Odio, Ekoong**, **Eka Ekpo, Akpan Ekpo, Okpo Record**, **Afai Ekpo**, **Nnabo**

The *Ijele m*asquerade originated in Anambra state is known as the "King of all masquerades." In ancient times, it had 45 masquerades perform on top of it, which are now represented by 45 figures. It was also used to scare away some of the early missionaries in Igboland. Masquerades made their way into the Diaspora, and can still be seen in modified forms in the Caribbean Carnival celebrations:

The Ejagham have two different types of women's masquerades; Ekpa masquerades reveal the dancer's identity, and Agot masquerades conceal it. However, it is most likely that the use of masks by women has been a site of controversy between the genders. And, how women have negotiated this performance strategy is not entirely clear. It may be a result of the powerful role that women, such as those in the Ekpa association, play in the ritual life of the Ejagham.

During festive daytime performances, an Ekpa woman will dance with an elaborately carved headdress mask that sits on top of her head, fastened with strings, allowing her face to be seen. The masks may look slightly different from place to place, depending upon the carver and the stylistic preferences in the region. The main components appear to be the representation of multiple faces or figures, the use of mirrors, the use of scarves or cloth, and the use of colorful pigments or paints. In a documented case in Cameroon, the main figure represents a woman with a snake, who is understood in many parts of Africa and the world as Mami Wata. However, in this case, the figure represents a female ancestor and the powers associated with her that give Ekpa women their power (Roschenthaler 1998).

Aside from the masked dances, Ekpa women also perform nighttime displays in which women sing, dance, and communicate with the spirit realm. Men are forbidden to witness these events, which may occur on a regular basis or may be called upon because of special circumstances (such as in the event of a war).

On the most serious of occasions, the women perform completely naked. In this context, the naked female body has a symbolic power that is associated with female sexuality and reproduction, whose meanings are deeply rooted in an Ejagham philosophy and worldview.

Both the Ekpa and the Agot women's masquerades comment upon, or satirize, male behavior. Describing an Ekpa performance in Cameroon, Ute Roschenthaler writes,

> The dance group, composed of at least nine women, appears. Some of them imitate and satirize typical male roles to the delight of the spectators: two or four "guards" run around carrying swords and machetes to control the dance floor; the "protocol leader" shakes his rattle; the "hunter's dog" searches for prey; the "soldier" points his gun at the audience; the "policemen" (called "blue bottoms") frighten with their large rods.[149]

Ekpe Masquerades in Igboland are known as mmanwu:

[149] https://kwekudee-tripdownmemorylane.blogspot.com/2013/06/ibibio-peoplethe-most-ancient-nigerian.html

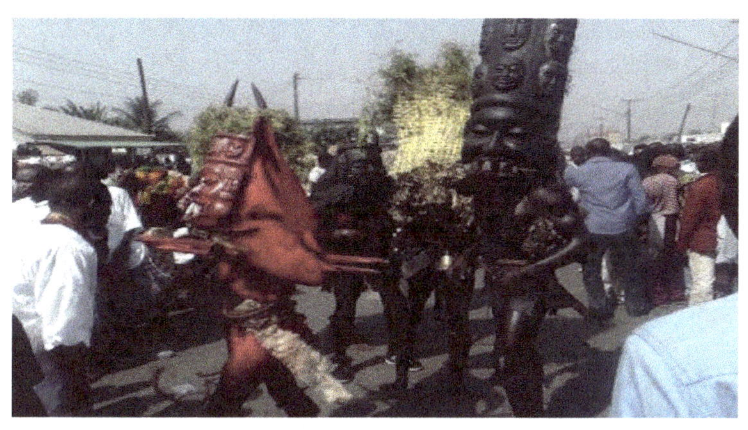

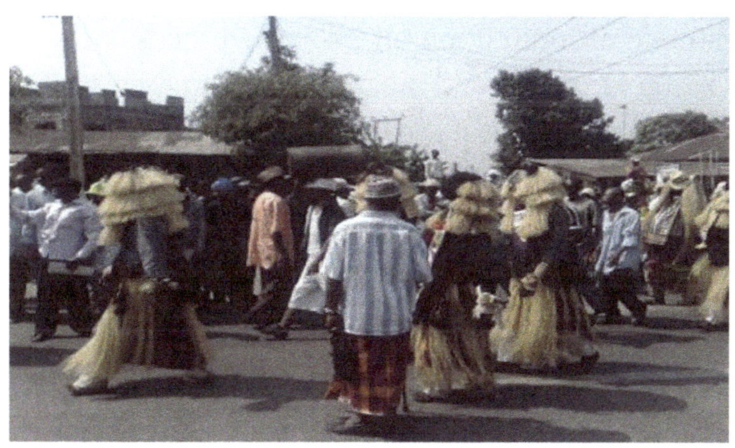

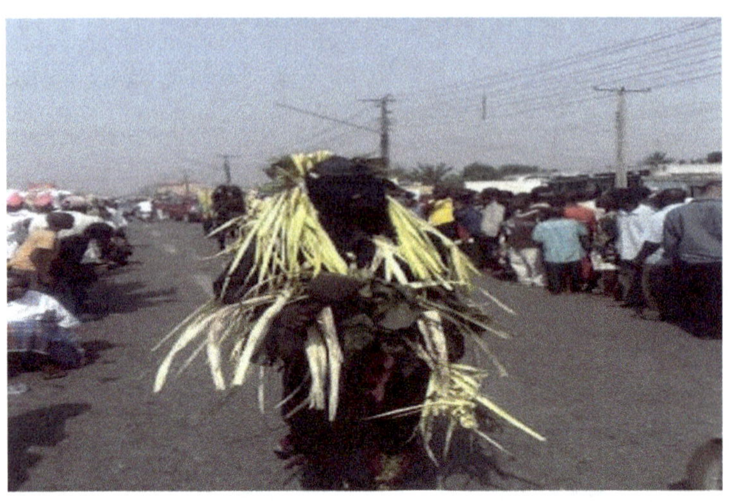

An important aspect of the *nsibidi* system involves encoding signs with an element of indirection. The aesthetic of indirection refers to the process of twisting language and meaning so as to conceal knowledge. Therefore, *nsibidi* can at times resemble a trick or a riddle. Talbot writes that "the Ekoi [or the Ejagham] explanation of the name nsibidi, or more properly Nchibbidy, is that it is derived from the verb *nchibbi,* 'to turn,' and this has taken to itself the meaning of agility of mind, and therefore of cunning or double meaning". For example, when Ekpa women give the sign for "talk," it actually means "don't talk." Non initiates would therefore be tricked into doing the wrong thing.

Individual signs often have multiple layers of meaning that may change over time and are affected by the context in which it is displayed. For example, one of the most popular signs is composed of two linking semicircles, one semicircle symbolizing a man and the other symbolizing a woman. As it appears on ancient carved stone monoliths, this sign probably referred to the combining of male and female reproductive forces—an important concept within ritual systems that ensured the fertility of the community in terms of agriculture and children. In contemporary times, this sign continues to signify the male and female union. A woman may tattoo this sign on her upper arm, which she would use to cradle her lover. Here, the design signifies the contemporary concept of "romantic love." Several creative individuals have inscribed the symbol onto wedding bands, incorporating the sign into a Western-based concept of marriage.[150]

Scholars believe that nsibidi originated among the Ejagham, who use it more extensively than any other group in the region. The spread of nsibidi may have been a result of Ejagham migrations or their practice of selling the secrets of the Ejagham men's Leopard Society (Ngbe) to their neighbors (the Igbo, Efik, Ibibio, Efut, Banyang, and others).

---

[150] African Folklore: An Encyclopedia edited by Philip M. Peek, Kwesi Yankah

In 1904, T.D.Maxwell, a British colonial officer, recognized the writing system, which soon became an interest of other Westerners as well. Other reports of nsibidi appeared at the beginning of the twentieth century by European missionaries, colonial officers, and ethnographers. Scholars believe that nsibidi is very old, but it is difficult to determine exactly when it began. Similar signs that appear on carved stone monoliths (possibly created as early as 200 CE) may provide a clue. Nsibidi is an esoteric form of knowledge that can only be fully understood by a select group of people. Various secret societies utilize this system to guard information that can only be known by its members through lengthy processes of initiation that may take a lifetime. While the meanings of these signs are often secret, the signs may be seen by the general public. Some of the most well-known examples of nsibidi have been produced by the male Leopard Society. Leopard Society members, who pursue excellence and expertise in the artistic and intellectual facets of nsibidi, create brilliant displays with their secret knowledge, which once gave them the power to enforce the laws of the society at large.[151]

Nsibidi has proven to be an adaptable and fluid

[151] https://africa.si.edu/exhibits/inscribing/nsibidi.html

system, capable of meeting the needs of changing times and circumstances. Expanding beyond the Cross River region of Africa, *nsibidi* use was brought to Cuba via the trans-Atlantic slave trade and into America along the paths of former slaves. In these new contexts, *nsibidi* flourished among the Abakua, a Cuban version of the Ejagham Leopard Society. More recently, *nsibidi* has been used by contemporary artists in the international arena. Artists in Nigeria, Cuba, and the United States have incorporated these signs and infused them in clothing and art.[152]

The structural resemblance between the Nsibidi pictograms of the Efik country (southeastern Nigeria) and Egyptian pictograms was recognized and reported as early as 1912 by an English scholar, P. Amaury Talbot. Many Egyptian hieroglyphs still show a distinct structural affinity to the signs used in the Mende script in southern Sierra Leone, and the same is true of most of the signs used in the Loma script in northern Liberia. There is also an undoubted causal connection between Egyptian hieroglyphs and several of the

---

[152] Slogar, Christopher (Spring 2007). "Early Ceramics from Calabar, Nigeria: Towards a History of Nsibidi". *African Arts*. University of California. **40** (1): 18–
29. doi:10.1162/afar.2007.40.1.18. S2CID 57566625.

signs used in the Vai script in the neighborhood of Monrovia (Liberia).

The Nsibidi symbols symbolize ideas on several levels of discourse. First there were signs most people knew regardless of initiation or rank in the Ngbe/Ekpe society, signs representing human relationships, communication, and household objects.

Shaded signs are signs of danger even as drums of silence announcing the death of an important Ngbe/Ekpe member were half shaded black and white. The black stood for the mud and death. The white stood for water, freshness, and vitality. This alludes to the Ekpe proverb" Where there's mud there must be water".

Mbufari Nsibidi patterns reflect the status of a woman who derives it and the status of her husband. She must have the proper training to use the correct colors for they are important symbolism. Example white means peace, red is equaling, green meaning plants, gold meaning light of the sun and blue if their husband has hopes of being a fisherman.[153]

---

[153] Amanda B. Carlson; In the Spirit and in the Flesh: Women, Masquerades, and the Cross River. *African Arts* 2019; 52 (1): 46–61. doi:

The head of the Ekpe pantheon is named Abasi Ibom. Abasi is known to have wanted a relationship with humans but due to humans lying to him he decided against it and in true Afrikan deity fashion he orphaned man and left the Ndem in his place. The lesser deities are named *N*dem and serve their ancestors as necessary intermediaries between the Creator and men. The Ndem are regarded as territorial in character as they are believed to reside in several areas in the lower Cross River. the Ndem include Udominyan, Anansa, Atabrinyang, Atakpor Uruan Inyang, Afianwan, Ekpenyong, Ekanem and several others.[154]

As Ndem are primarily marine deities, most of its emblems are aquatic creatures. Among these creatures include python, alligator, and crocodile. The species of Crocodile known in the Efik language as Fiom Nkọi represents Atabrinyang, a deity believed to reside at Effiat. The black kite is regarded as the messenger of Atakpor Uruan. Marriages are also believed to occur among the Ndem. Anansa Ikang Obutong is believed to be the spouse of Anantigha Enwang. Atakpor Uruan is also believed to be the spouse of Atabrinyang.

---

[154] *Essien, Dominic (1993), Uruan people in Nigerian history, Uyo: Modern business press Ltd.,* ISBN 9782676217

Other unions between Ndem include Obo and Eme; Ebebe and Ukọñ Esụk.[155][156][157]

[155] *Simmons, Donald C. (1958). Analysis of the Reflection of Culture in Efik folktales (PhD). Yale University.*

[156] *Talbot, Percy Amaury (1923),* Life in Southern Nigeria; the magic, beliefs, and customs of the Ibibio tribe, *London: Macmillan and Co.* OCLC 1687947

[157] *Etifit, Edet Solomon (1979). Aspects of the Pre-Colonial History of Enwang in Oron Local Government Area (BA). University of Nigeria, Nsukka.*

NGOMA

We will now take a trip down south to our brothers most known as the Zulus where they practice a system known as Ngoma. Ngoma is said to mean drum and the naming of the entire spiritual system of this instrument denotes the importance of the drum amongst the Zulu spiritual practices. The priest of this tradition is known as Sangoma. Sangoma loosely translates to man of the drum again denoting the importance of the drum but also denoting a skilled priest must be familiar with to have such a title. One way drumming is used is to incite and call forth spirits and ancestors during ritual festival and initiations. Like the old saying goes in Afrika without the drum there is no ritual. Another definition of Sangoma is those that do Ngoma. According to Sangoma and author of the book Zulu Shaman Vusamazulu Credo Mutwa says that Sangoma's are called to the tradition by developing a strange unexplainable sickness. This sickness is only treatable by becoming a full-fledged Sangoma and if not identified as such the person called can die.[158] Sangoma are said to learn how to heal the community in a variety of ways. One of the ways is a form of what would probably be described as some type of psychology by

---

[158] Zulu Shaman Dreams Prophecies and Mysteries by Vusamazulu Credo Mutwa

western standards. For example, Credo Mutwa says if a person is having hallucinations about an imaginary dog attacking them it's the Sangoma's job to punish the dog to calm the patient. Sangoma also deal in divination for the community. When they are going through initiation a calf or goat is slaughtered. Afterward the bladder of the animal is inflated and must be worn by the initiate in the hair. This signifies to the spirits he or she they are ready to communicate. There is a saying that alludes to this ritual in Zulu land. It is said that diviners have soft heads. This may be a metaphor for the bladder, but I also think it symbolizes the head being soft enough to be influenced and communicated with. If the head is hard, it is set and cannot be changed. The bones of that calf or goat are cleaned and carved and given to the Sangoma.[159] They are called Dingaka and they are known as oracle bones. These are the divination tools of the Sangoma and although the generic name is dingaka they are broken into different categories named lekwami meaning old man, kgadi meaning old woman, selume meaning young man, and koatsane meaning young woman. When the bones are facing upwards after being casted, they are smiling and when they are facing

---

[159] Zulu Shaman Dreams Prophecies and Mysteries by Vusamazulu Credo Mutwa

downwards, they are sleeping.[160] Within Ngoma, they have pictographs like the Dogon, Akan and Ancient Egyptians. The meanings are imbedded in the mythology of the system.

---

[160] Zulu Shaman Dreams Prophecies and Mysteries by Vusamazulu Credo Mutwa

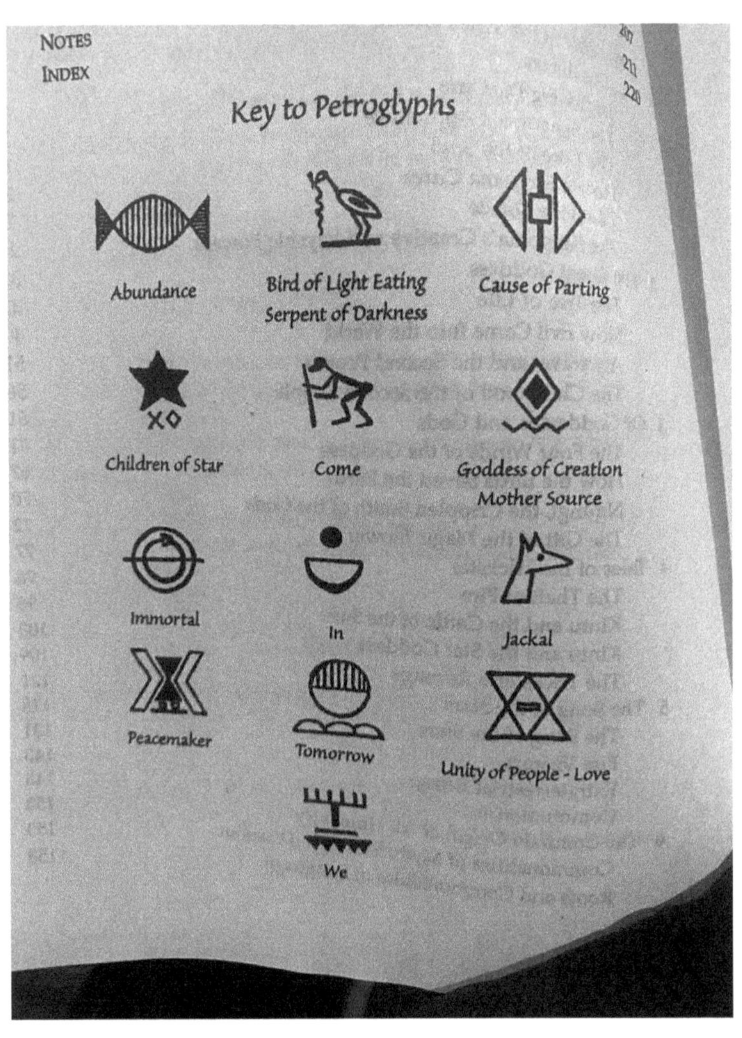

The Ngoma head of the pantheon is called Unkulukulu known as the great spirit.[161] According to Asar Imhotep this word linguistically means "the oldest of the old" and is often referred to us as "our primary ancestor." The oldest ancestor would

[161] Indaba My Children by Vusamazulu Credo Mutwa

be the Creator itself which is the totality of existence in African societies.[162] According to Zulu mythology Unkulukulu is a star being ancestor who came from the stars and found the ancient Zulus living like animals and without laws. He taught them to build huts and taught them the high laws of isiNtu.[163] Unkulukulu may also be a corruption of the original name for this deity Ukhulukhulwana or UkhuluKhukwan.[164] The Ngoma tradition have many deities, but we will cover a few of them.

Nomhoyi, the deity of rivers and queen of old and decay and ruler of the under world

Nomkhubulwane Deity of the rainbow, agriculture, rain, and beer

Kintu the trickster divinity

Sonzwaphi the deity of healing

---

[162] AKAN AND EGYPTIAN SYMBOL COMPARISONS: PART 1 By Asar Imhotep Monday December 20, 2010 The MOCHA-Versity Institute of Philosophy and Research

[163] https://www.encyclopedia.com/environment/encyclopedias-almanacs-transcripts-and-maps/zulu-religion

[164] https://www.encyclopedia.com/environment/encyclopedias-almanacs-transcripts-and-maps/zulu-religion

Umvelinqangi (meaning "He who was in the very beginning"), God of thunder and earthquakes.

Ma or ninhavanhu-Ma first female deity of Ngoma and Mother Earth

Somaga Sun God

Nyanaga the moon

Ntontozayo great bull

Sixaxa earth tortoise. Carries earth on his back around the sun

Nkanyamba python of the universe (Eats himself to show infinity)

Ngungi God of Iron

Simba kade tree of life

Amarava deity that birthed Khoisan and Twa Afrikan tribes[165][166]

---

[165] Zulu Shaman Dreams Prophecies and Mysteries by Vusamazulu Credo Mutwa

[166] https://www.encyclopedia.com/environment/encyclopedias-almanacs-transcripts-and-maps/zulu-religion

PORRO/SANDE

We must now go back west to Sierra Leone and parts of Liberia to look at two systems that come from the same people. The Mande people of various ethnic groups have a system for teaching boys to be men and girls to be women. These systems are called Porro and Sande respectfully. Porro is the authoritative factor that a male must go through in order to be considered a full tribal member. The main function of the Porro society is to guarantee a good relationship between the living world and the ancestors. The system basically teaches you not only to be a man but to be human by the tribal standard. It's also associated with hunting, and I think this is because of the strictly male element. The society is so influential that even when babies are born, they are temporarily granted admission until they grow of agc and can go through the full initiation.[167] The men that carry out this ritual take young boys to the forest to carry out a series of rituals. The elders of the society must feel to boy has matured and is able to keep the secrets of the society; the consequences of break to pact of secrecy is death. Before the initiation ritual the boy goes through a series of lesson teaching him, they ways of becoming a

[167] Mossi Warrior Clan Present Spearitual Combat A historical Survey of The Minds of African Warrior Scholars Vol 3

man. Some tribe's non-members are required to stay in their homes away from the ritual. In the initiation the boy undergoes physical torture in order to "be killed by the spirits" and is then reborn a man. The physical process usually includes circumcision and given tribal markings (usually leaving deep scars). The initiation covers a 7-year period and usually begins at the time of puberty. It is rumored to be 99 phases of this initiation. Only at the end of the initiation process are the initiates deemed ready for marriage.[168][169] In their work The Dances of Africa, Michael Huet and Claude Savary explain the initiatory phases of the Senufo of the Ivory Coast (Sinematyali, Korbogo, and Bundyali regions). The first phase is the junior class (*plaga*, *plawo*, *nyara*) or Poro for children between 7 and 12 years of age. The second age group (*tyenungo*, *nayogo*, *kwonro*) is for boys between 12 and 18 years of age, which proceeds from the initiatory phase of the sacred wood (*tyologo*) and completes the young men's training after age 18. When the initiates return

---

[168] Alterman, O., Binienda, A., Rodella, S., and Varzi, K. (2002) *The Law People See: The Status of Dispute Resolution in the Provinces of Sierra Leone in 2002*, A National Forum for Human Rights Publication. http://www.daco-sl.org/encyclopedia/8_lib/8_3/research/lawpeoplesee.pdf

[169] Ibid; Minority Rights Group International, World Directory of Minorities and Indigenous Peoples; Sierra Leone Overview, http://www.minorityrights.org/4807/sierra-leone/sierra-leone-overview.html (11-12)

from the sacred wood, their initiation is complete. Then public ceremonies, tantamount to modern-day graduation, take place.[170] People who have not been initiated are called *kp*owa (literally "fool, insane, deranged"), whereas members of the Poro and Sande societies are known as *halemo*. An initiate in training is referred to as a mbogdoni.[171]

Although it is a rites of passage ceremony it's also a spiritual teaching and practical instruction period. This usually takes place in the dry season between October and May.[172] The spirits of secret societies are Represented in the form of carved wooden masks. For example, at the time of her initiation into the Sande society, a female receives a mask that was carved specially for her by the woodcarver following specific instructions received during a dream. As a sacred object, a mask must be kept in a hidden place. When it is worn, such as during initiation ceremonies, the rest of the body must be covered with raffia fibers, with the mask resting over the head and shoulders. Sande masks (also known as Bondu masks)

---

[170] Molefi Asante and Ama Azama Encyclopedia of African Religion
[171] Alterman, O., Binienda, A., Rodella, S., and Varzi, K. (2002) *The Law People See: The Status of Dispute Resolution in the Provinces of Sierra Leone in 2002*, A National Forum for Human Rights Publication. http://www.daco-sl.org/encyclopedia/8_lib/8_3/research/lawpeoplesee.pdf
[172] Mossi Warrior Clan Present Spearitual Combat A historical Survey of The Minds of African Warrior Scholars Vol 3

usually have the shape of conical helmets. They represent the only case known in Africa of masks exclusively reserved for women.[173]

[173] Molefi Asante and Ama Azama Encyclopedia of African Religion

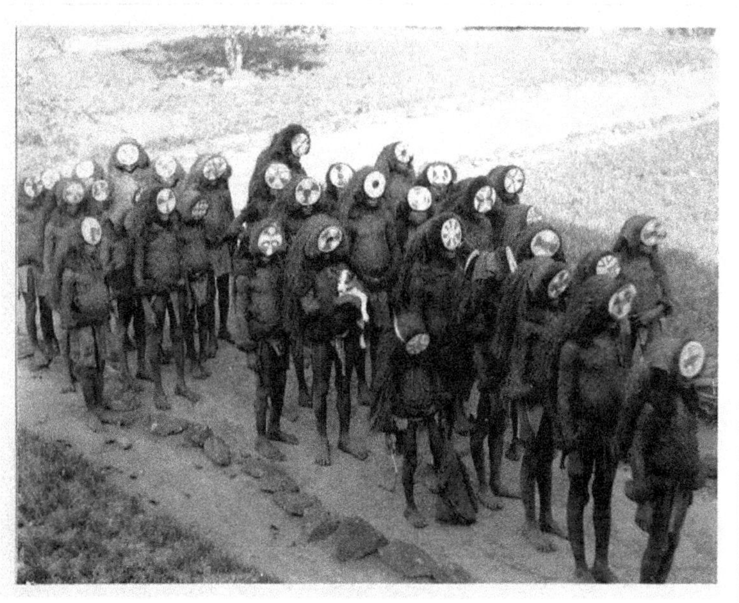

Boys returning from their initiation in the Poro. Panguma, Sierra Leone (Photo: Sjoerd Hofstra, 1936)

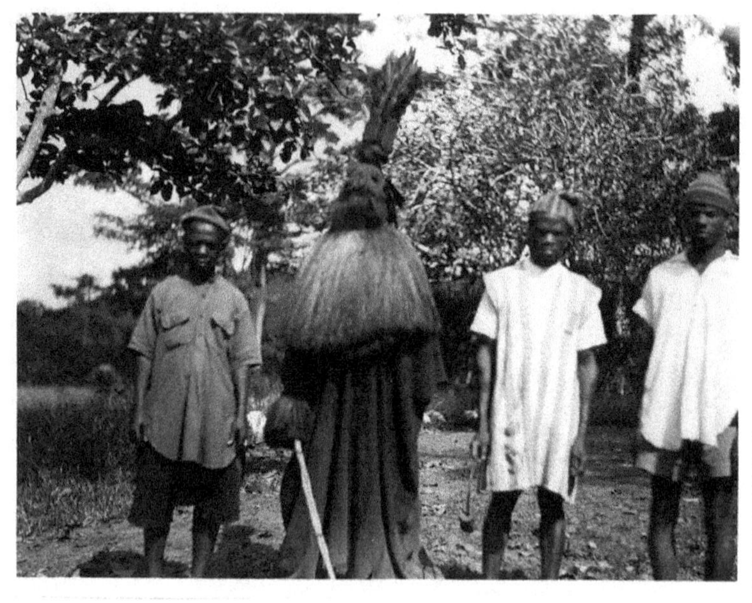

A "falui" masker, a one-armed warrior spirit. Panguma, Sierra Leone.

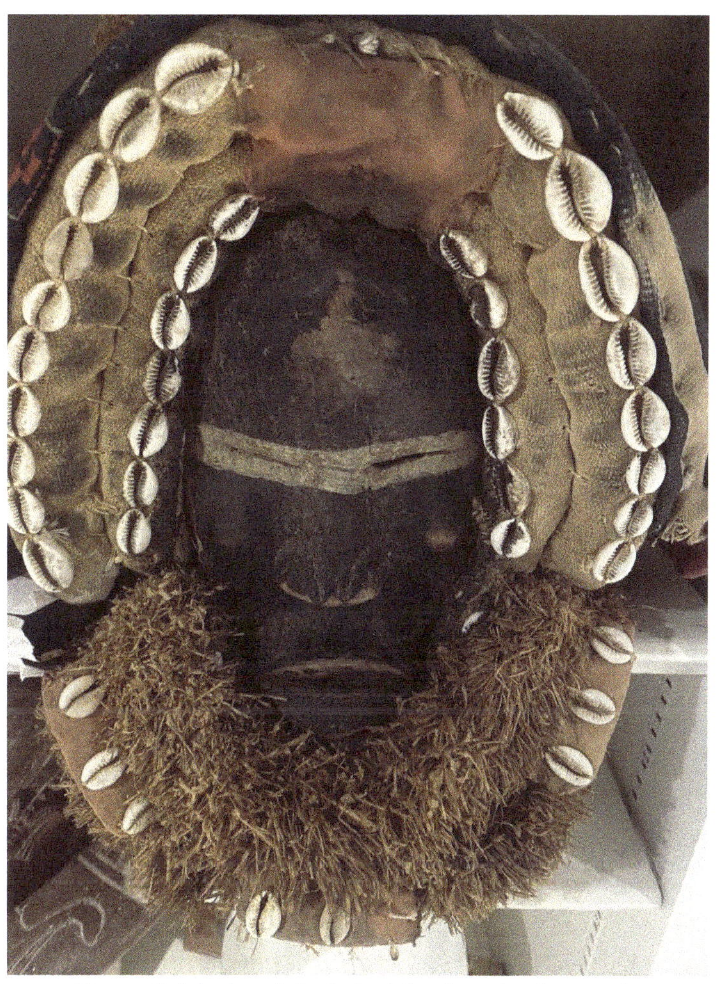

Porro Initiation Mask I picked up in Senegal.

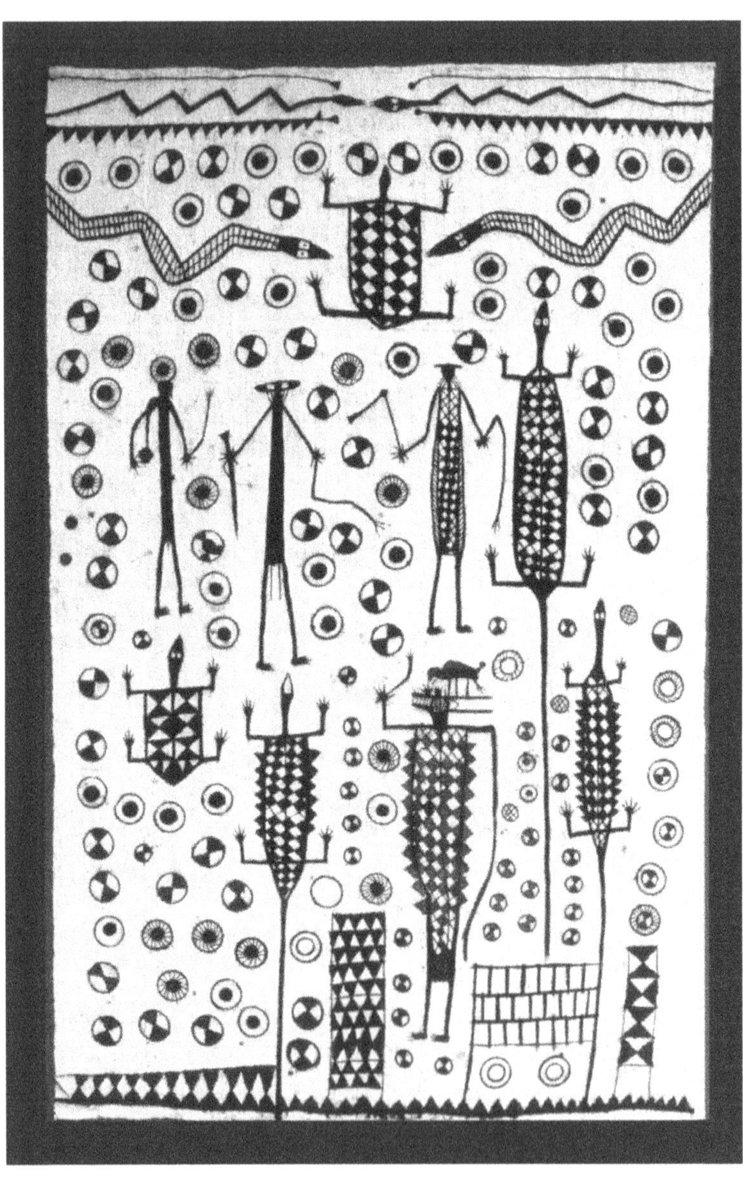

Painted cloth costume worn by Senufo Poro society masquerader. Similar cloths were also worn by hunters. The designs, regarded as protective, are painted onto locally woven narrow strip cloth using green paint made from boiled leaves, then outlined with a mud solution. Senufo, Ivory Coast. Source: Werner Forman/Art Resource, New York.

Sande is the system in the same region for women and young girls. This system is also sometimes called Bondo. Sande also takes on a political nature as many women who have run for office in Sierra Leone have been required to take this undertaking. Just like in Porro there is a death element in Sande. The little girls symbolically must die to become a woman. The river the first stop instead of the Forrest. The river is used in many Afrikan initiations to symbolizes washing away the old and being born a new. Water, for example, is regarded as the origin of life. The river is regarded as the place of crossing from the village to the forest and vice versa. Crossing the river relates to all sorts of crossings; in death, for example, the deceased is said to cross the river to the otherworld, or in the resurrection of the masked spirit of a-Nowo, who is fetched from beyond the water. A zigzag line, the hieroglyph for water all over Africa, is written on the forehead of the Nöwo mask.[174] The girls then go to the Forrest

[174] Molefi Asante and Ama Azama Encyclopedia of African Religion

for instruction. They are instructed on how to be women and by that instruction and more they are transformed into something different from when they entered. They are given new names and are sisters for life. Some of the skills they learn are farming, dying clothes, domestic duties, dancing, medicine and even sexual education.[175] New initiates enter and remain in the sacred forest for a period that can range from a few months to 1 year. Hojo—white clay, kaolin, or porcelain clay—is found in the riverbed and at the riverside. The highest quality of hojo is found in the riverbed and is the most difficult to obtain. Initiates paint their faces, and in some rural areas, they paint their entire bodies white with hojo. Hojo is the highest ideals of beauty, perfection, and goodness. For Sande/Bondo, white is significant because the color is linked with the spirit world and with the secret parts of human society, where people strive for the highest spiritual and moral ideals. However, black indicates the metaphysical process of refinement and acculturation.[176] The graduation known as the "Pouring Out Ceremony" lasts for 2

---

[175] Mossi Warrior Clan Present Spearitual Combat A historical Survey of The Minds of African Warrior Scholars Vol 3

[176] Molefi Asante and Ama Azama Encyclopedia of African Religion

days.[177] With every ritualistic graduation event in Afrika it becomes a community event celebration.

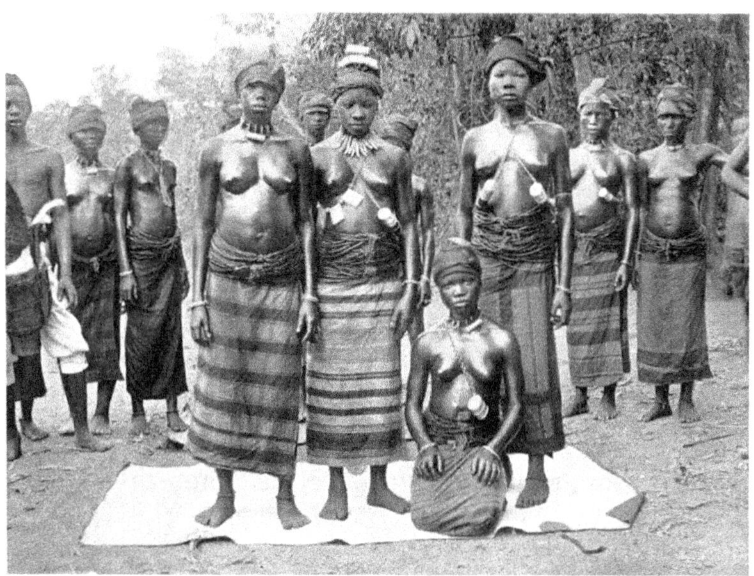

[177] Molefi Asante and Ama Azama Encyclopedia of African Religion

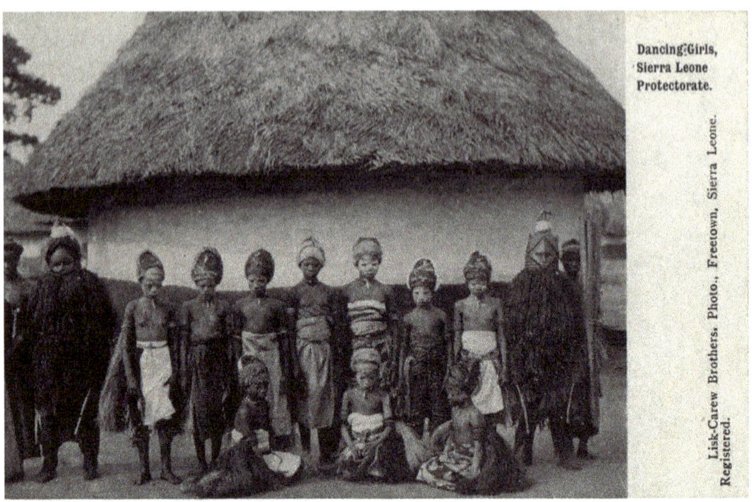

The primary ethnic group for these people is called the Temme and although there are many different Mande groups I could pick from I will pick this one to talk about their head of the pantheon. Its name is Kurumasaba and in true Afrikan fashion (you probably guessed it by now) the deity does not get involved in the affairs of man his task is left to the ancestors, who serve as the privileged intermediaries between God and the living. As a result, the ancestors are propitiated through numerous rituals, including sacrifices and offerings. The ancestors are expected to protect the living and send them many blessings, in particular children. Procreation and marriage are indeed of paramount importance. In addition to the ancestors, there exist other spiritual entities that may be helpful or harmful to people. Therefore, they too are offered sacrifices to appeal to or neutralize them (This should sound familiar by now).

ESULALU AWASENA

Let's go back to the Senegambia region to talk about an Afrikan spiritual system many have probably never heard of. This system is of the Diola, Koonjeaen and Esulalu people. The Diola or Jola people are an ethnic group of Senegambia and Guinea-Bassu. Esulalu is an area of five townships on the south shore of the Casamance river.[178] The Koonjean are the original people of this region live in compounds like most west Afrikans. When it comes to the spiritual system of this region there are 4 words that describe it. The first one is called Makanaye which means literally what we do. The people of this region don't have a concept of religion, just a way of life. The second term is called Boutine which literally means path. The third term is called Kainoe which literally means thought. The fourth term and the title of this chapter is Asawena which means one who performs rituals or follower of Diola spiritual traditions.[179] Each compound is called hank and has what is called Kalybillah which is the particular shrine and ritual rules. There are several different types of shrines dedicated to deities and

---

[178] Shrines of the Slave Trade Diola Religion And Society In Precolonial Senegambia by Robert N. Baum

[179] Shrines of the Slave Trade Diola Religion And Society In Precolonial Senegambia by Robert N. Baum

ancestors alike. The deity at the head of the pantheon name is Emitai. The name comes from the Diola word emit which means sky and year,[180] this denotes the strong relationship between the Diola people and farming. The sky provides the environmental conditions to have crops and the year denotes the agricultural year. Like most Afrikan deities he is aloof and does not interact with humans but with the syncretism of Christianity and Islam some are seeking to change that narrative. Traditional Kalybillah worship barely invokes the name Emitai in prayer. Oral traditions state that Emitai selected 10 men to introduce various types of spirit shrines and teaching to the Diola communities. The ones selected are said to be the first ancestors of the Diola people. The deities that the Diola pray to are called Sainaati, this is a general designation for spirit shrines. There are other shrines called Ukine. It is said that Emitai created Ukine to establish specific ways for individuals, families or communities seeking assistance in the resolution of problems. There are specific spirits used for specific things like Kasila which is a deity used to combat drought, Ehugna is a deity for fertility and

[180] Shrines of the Slave Trade Diola Religion And Society In Precolonial Senegambia by Robert N. Baum

Cabai was for war.[181] When one dies and lived a life according to the tradition, they were rewarded with the title of ancestor which in their language is Ahoeka, when one did not live their life in the correct manner according to the tradition, they were called Ahoelra which means phantom. This alludes to the age old Afrikan concept of being a wanderer on earth if one does not exude good character in life. There are three possible scenarios for the deceased according to Diola culture. The first is you become and Ahoeka and you live near your family compound, the second is you become a Ahoelra and wander until you eventually die and be reborn to have an attempt to live righteously again. The third is you are sent to what is called the Housandioume where you live much like you were when you were alive. You eventually die and are reborn. The Ahoeka are summoned at their shrine called Kouhouloung, this shrine reaches the place where the ancestors dwell called Kahoeka.[182] Through this shrine the Esulaulu people pay homage, ask questions, and even settle disputes. Many children are introduced to this shrine in a ritual called Kahit. The Kahit ritual entails of a child being presented to his ancestors and asking

---

[181] Shrines of the Slave Trade Diola Religion And Society In Precolonial Senegambia by Robert N. Baum

[182] Shrines of the Slave Trade Diola Religion And Society In Precolonial Senegambia by Robert N. Baum

those ancestors to protect the child and the child's animal double so that they may live a long life.[183] You may have seen this masquerade called Kumpo on the internet in recent years. The masquerade is dressed in palm leaves with a protruding stick-on top of its head. The masquerade spins on this stick much to the delight of the crowd in attendance. According to the tradition and like most Afrikan masquerades the Kumpo is not a person but a type of spirit. The person's identity that is carrying this spirit must not be revealed. He may not be touched, and it is considered taboo to look into the palm leaves. (This is the exact same theme that surrounds the Egúgún amongst the Yorùbá) Therefore, he defends himself against intruders with his stick by smashing and pointing(please see pic below).[184] The purpose of the mask is to protect Jola villages from bad supernatural forces, coordinate communal works and protect males during circumcision initiation rituals time when they are perceived to be at their most vulnerable.[185]

---

[183] Shrines of the Slave Trade Diola Religion And Society In Precolonial Senegambia by Robert N. Baum

[184] Gina Gertrud Smith, Stanislaw Grodz. *Religion, Ethnicity and Transnational Migration between West Africa and Europe*. p. 115.

[185] http://www.accessgambia.com/information/cultural-dance.html

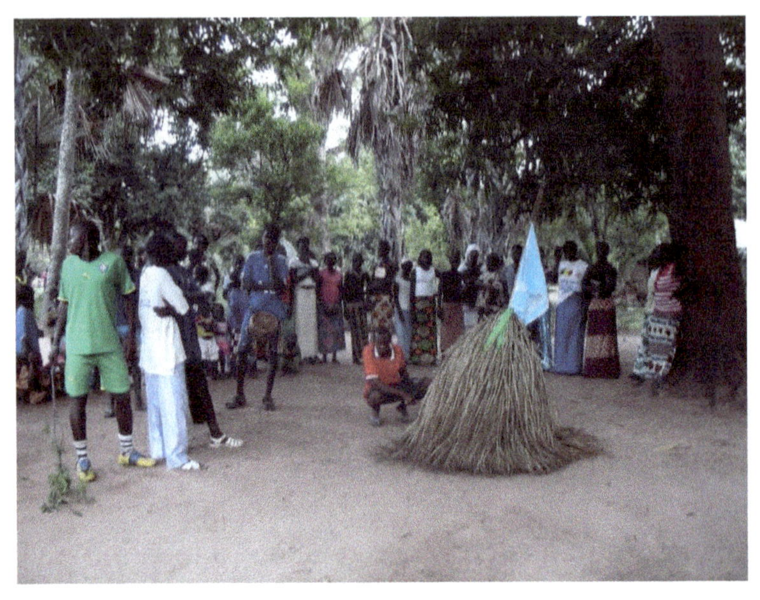

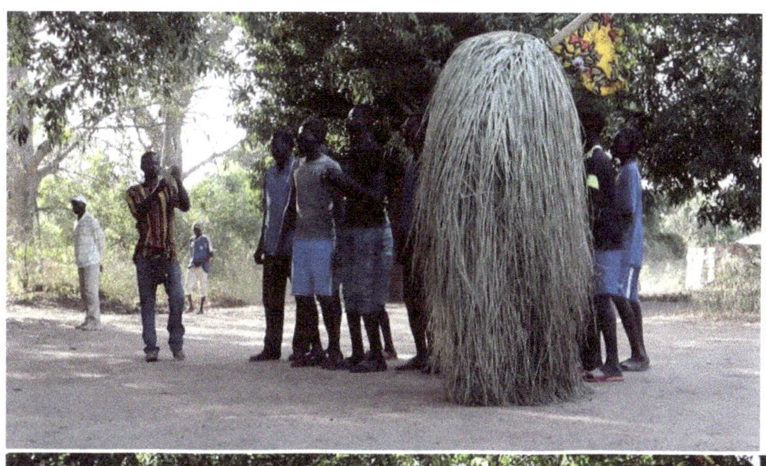

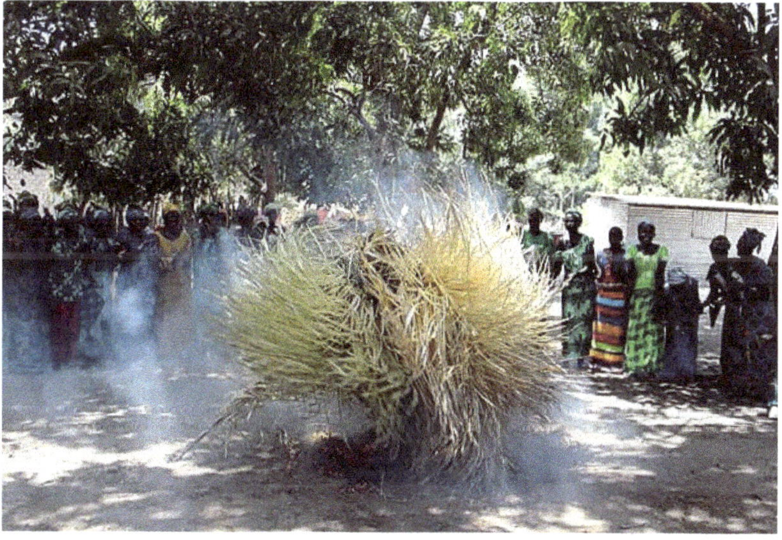

The other type of masquerades is called the Samay and Niasse. Little is known about these two masquerades but from what I have heard the Samay is the disciplinarian masquerade (see pic below). I could not find anything on the Niasse masquerade, but I do have a picture below.

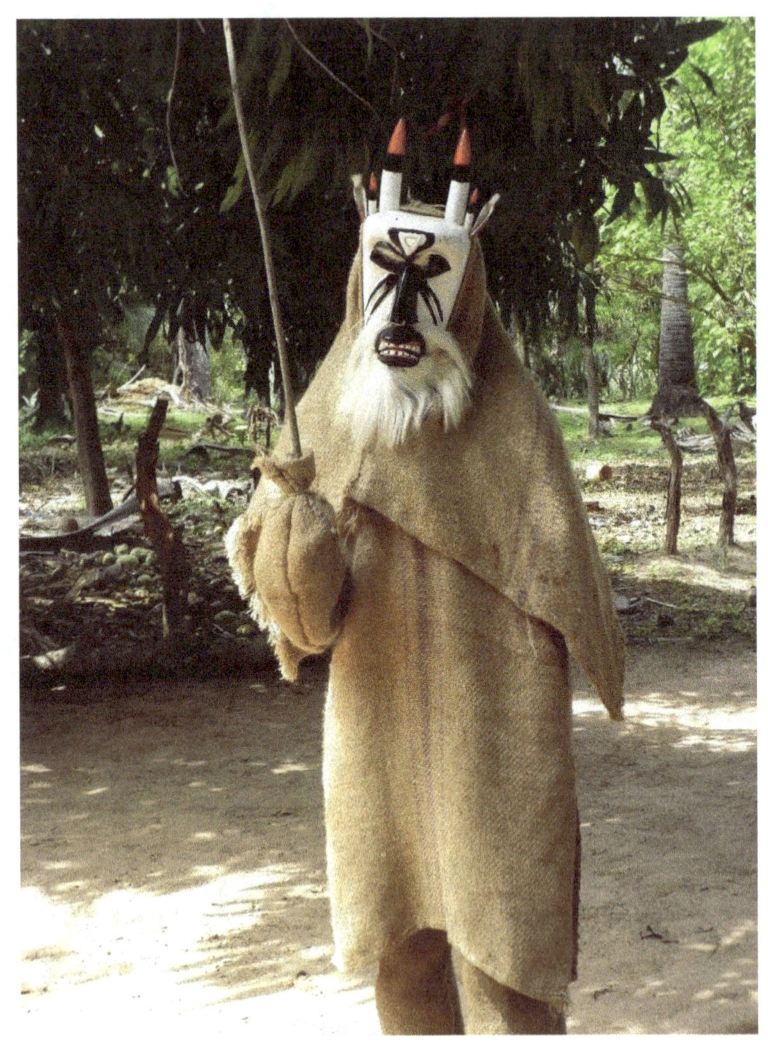

Samay

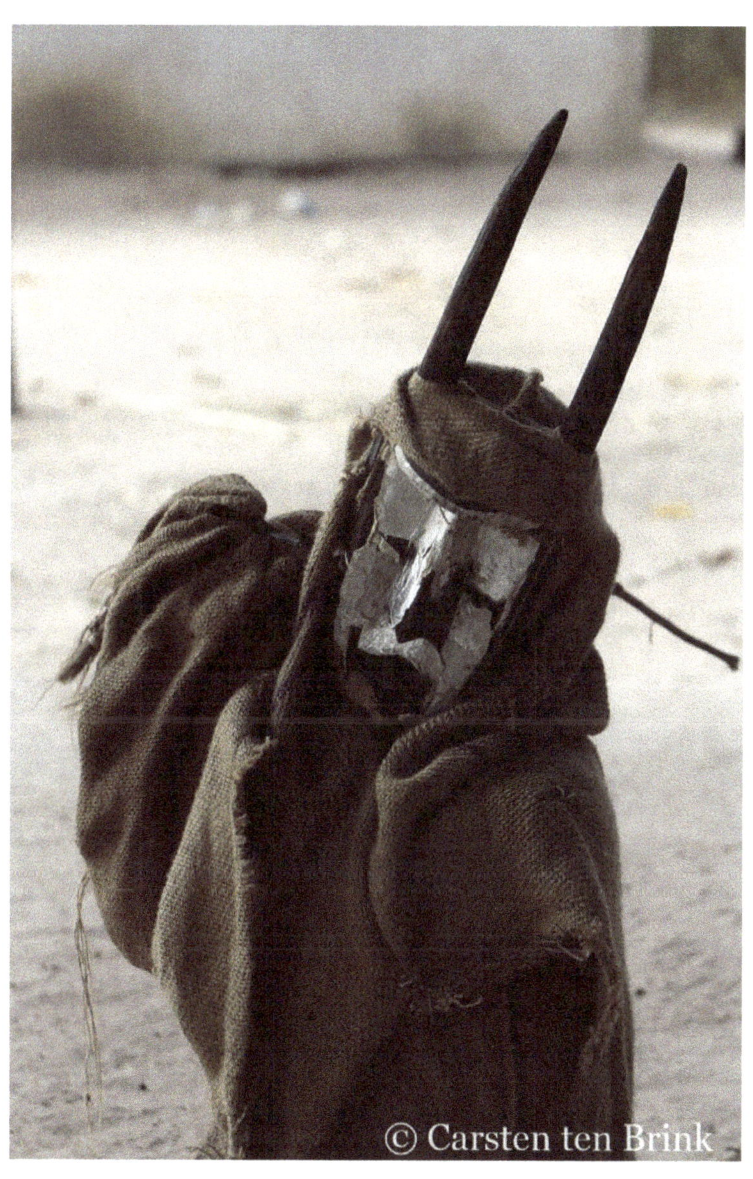

Samay

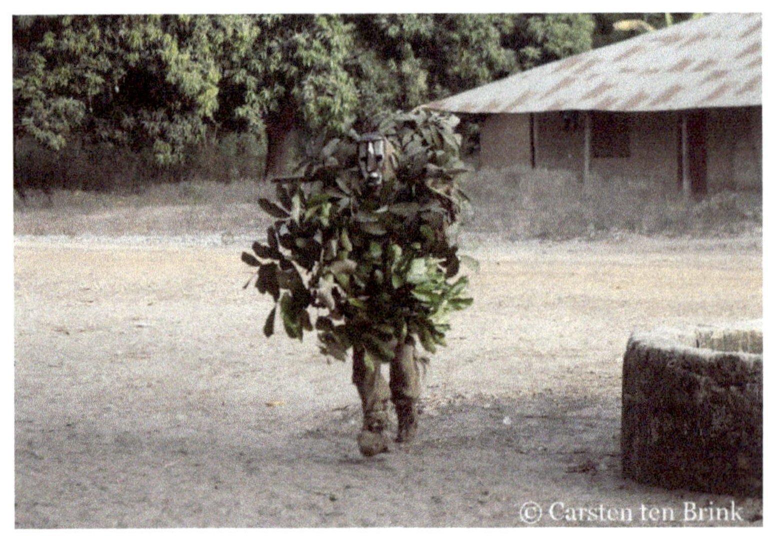

Niasse

Community and Spirituality

(community of memory)

Amadou Hampaté Bâ coined the following statement, which has achieved the level of African proverb: "When an elder dies, it is a library that burns down." This saying suggests that elders are regarded as knowledge-holders in communities of memory, and it is precisely for this reason that they are much sought after.[186] When we talk about Ki.môyo and Afrikan spiritual systems in general we must understand that the trained specialist or priest are not just individuals, we are a part of a collective consciousness of community based knowledge. It is our culture that unities our thoughts, morals, scruples, and identity. Long after we are gone the lessons of our cultural practices will continue and if that is true the community will thrive even in the absence of our physical form. Afrikan writer Wa Thiongo Ngugi in his writings seeks to demonstrate how African communities of memory have lost their moral understandings and commitments, which they need to recover for

---

[186] **Beyond the Colonial Gaze: Reconstructing African Wisdom Traditions**
A Dissertation submitted in partial satisfaction of the requirements for the degree of Doctor of Philosophy in Religious Studies by Kykosa Kajangu Committee in Charge: Professor Charles Long, Chair Professor Inès Talamantez Professor Barbara Holdrege June 2005

Afrikans to navigate once again in the river of their beginnings. It is in this river that Africans may enjoy spiritual renewal, which is the last theme of the return.[187] We must recover our cultural purpose through our ki.môyo, no foreign religion or practice can give us what we lost. What has been historically and presently stolen from us is the only vehicle that can take us to spiritual rejuvenation. We are in desperate need of a spiritual rejuvenation, with this rejuvenation comes improved character, medicinal knowledge, self-sustaining practices, family history, and access to power. Not just spiritual power but the political power as well. Could you imagine a United States of Afrika free of colonial religions, concepts, and debt? What type of world power would we be? When a Japanese man is harmed in any other part of the world but Japan his country gets involved. Think of what that would mean for Afrikans all over the world that get mistreated. Those of us that are interested and advocate the idea of spiritual renewal must have a clear understanding of the workings of African wisdom. It has been relatively

---

[187] **Beyond the Colonial Gaze: Reconstructing African Wisdom Traditions**
A Dissertation submitted in partial satisfaction of the requirements for the degree of Doctor of Philosophy in Religious Studies by Kykosa Kajangu Committee in Charge: Professor Charles Long, Chair Professor Inès Talamantez Professor Barbara Holdrege June 2005

easy for African postcolonial thinkers to develop counter-hegemonic texts, but it has been difficult for them to produce visionary texts because of their limited training in pre- Western modes of thought and being.[188] Culture defends itself when exercised correctly. When the tents of the community are activated, they perform functions that benefit the community. This chart below from the great Dr. Fukiau shows a great example of my point.

---

[188] **Beyond the Colonial Gaze: Reconstructing African Wisdom Traditions**
A Dissertation submitted in partial satisfaction of the requirements for the degree of Doctor of Philosophy in Religious Studies by Kykosa Kajangu Committee in Charge: Professor Charles Long, Chair Professor Inès Talamantez Professor Barbara Holdrege June 2005

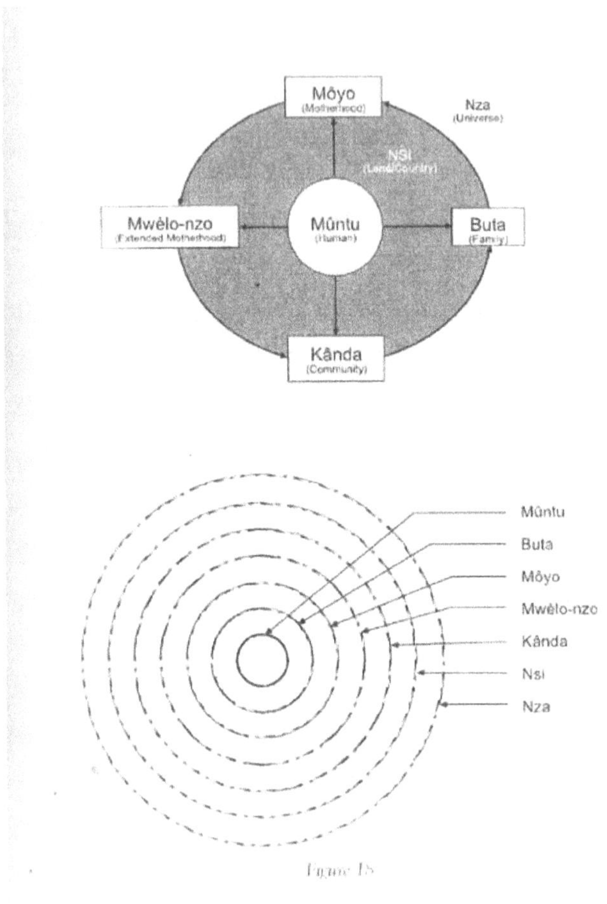

Figure 18

Whether one realizes it or not this is two protection systems inside of the Kongolese culture. Up top you have the Muntu in the middle. Muntu is a Kongolese word for human. Above Muntu you have Môyo which is the root word in ki.môyo but in this instance it means motherhood. To the left you have mwèlo-nzo which is the extended motherhood, these could be related women or non-related women. To the right you have bula meaning family, below you have kânda and yes this is the same word in Wakanda, and it means community. Lastly out of the circle is nza meaning universe. Do you see how all these cultural and family elements protect the induvial? This is what traditional Afrikan culture does when exercised properly, it forms a barrier of protection from threats. The second drawing is the same but presented differently. Notice the circles inside of circles, the circles denote that each element is a system and systems inside of systems create power. Systems inside of systems create memories and the community keeps these memories as lessons for practical application. Once we peel back the layers to this cultural onion and receive the training to be specialist in areas of the community, we restore the memory from our ancestors and begin to write a new. The literacy of initiation is achieved through the mastery of the sacred arts of a community of memory. In participatory research the researcher works in a center of wisdom in which he or she receives practical training in the sacred arts to acquire the double sight. Malidoma Somé describes the practical training to acquire the literacy of initiation. Traditional education consists of three parts: enlargement of one's ability to see, destabilization of the body's habit of being bound to one plane of being, and the ability to voyage transdimensionaly and return. Enlarging one's vision and abilities has nothing supernatural about it; rather, it is "natural" to be part of nature and to participate in a wider understanding of reality.[189] Our dearly departed brother Malidoma is describing what the Dagara people gain from initiation and traditional education. When you think about one's ability to see think about who's lens you are using to see. Is it your ancestors or is it the colonial thugs that enslaved them? Are you contributing to the community of memory or helping to erase it? My brother Asar Imhotep talks about the Afrikan super information highway in which learned priest traveled to lands far and wide to bring back knowledge. This is part explains why similar practices are in different parts of Afrika. They expanded their knowledge and enhanced their community's memory. Is this a practice we have abandoned today? Do we no longer see the benefit in knowledge? We are not unique in the sense that we are the only people that have communities of memory. Every race of people

---

[189] **Beyond the Colonial Gaze: Reconstructing African Wisdom Traditions**
A Dissertation submitted in partial satisfaction of the requirements for the degree of Doctor of Philosophy in Religious Studies by Kykosa Kajangu Committee in Charge: Professor Charles Long, Chair Professor Inès Talamantez Professor Barbara Holdrege June 2005

engages in this practice and make sure to teach their younger generations the lesson from the past. Why do we as Afrikan people act as if we are exempt and let our libraries burn to the ground?

Conclusion

We have covered a lot of topics in this publication and given elaborate examples to include scholastic references, Afrikan oracular utterances, pictures, and contextual analysis to illustrate different points. I did my best to provide as much evidence as I could, I am a firm believer that evidence should stand on its own. Ki.môyo is so vast, multifaceted and unique that it could never be categorized within the simplistic design of religion. Religion was not designed with the Afrikan in mind. Comfortability is easier than accuracy and efficiency takes a back seat to effort. We cannot continue to be comfortable with effort, but we must be accurate and efficient. This is the path to sovereignty, freedom, autonomy, and self-sustainability. We must apply this not only to scientific achievements but to the investigation of our spiritual culture and ancient ways of life. We will do nothing but benefit from preserving and upholding these traditions. The Afrikan race has benefitted nothing from foreign religions but chattel slavery, sub servitude, misplacement, and debt. It is time the children of the diaspora learn and lead the charge to return to our ancient practices to create a new vision with old perspectives. Ki.môyo is the future as well as the past and the present. Àlàáfíà, Amandla, and Abibifahodie (Health, Power, and Afrikan Liberation).

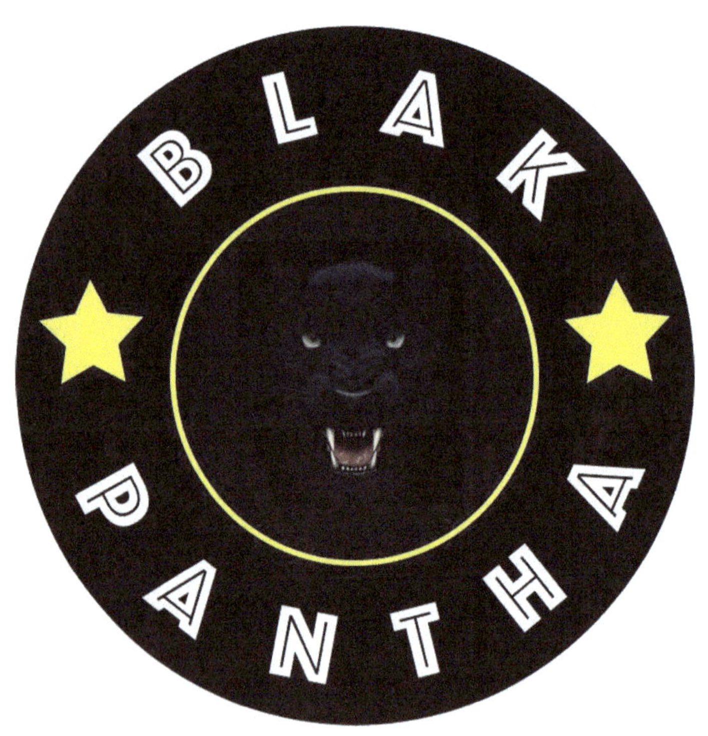
BLAK
PANTHA

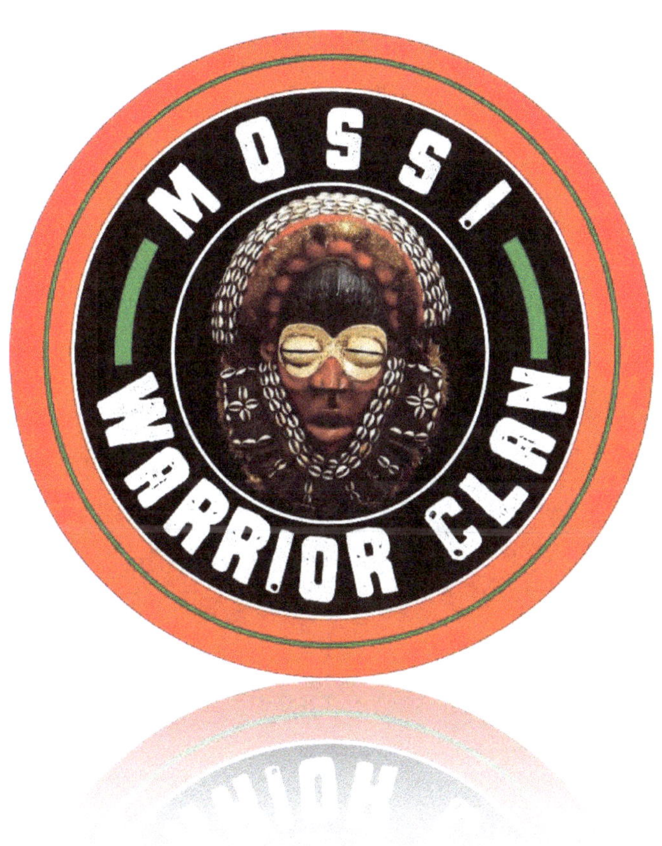
MOSSI
WARRIOR CLAN

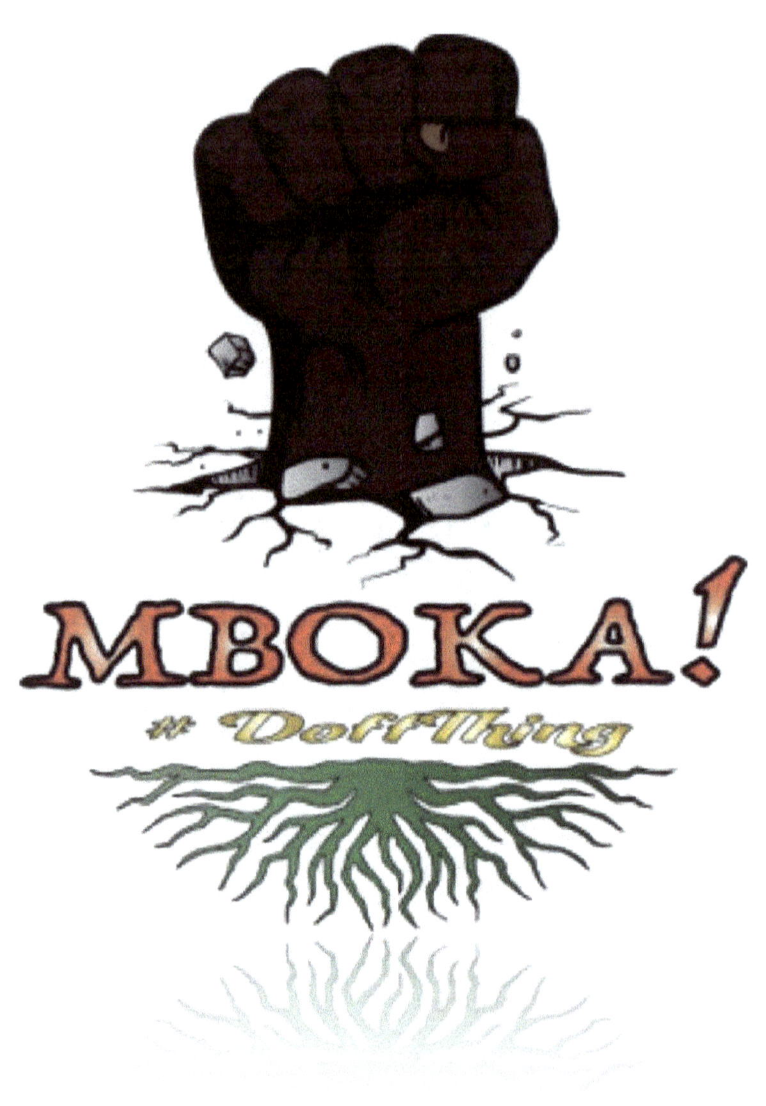
MBOKA!
DeffThing

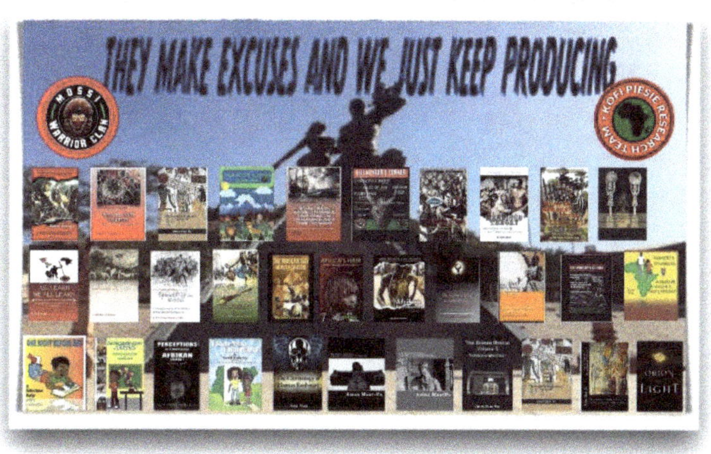
THEY MAKE EXCUSES AND WE JUST KEEP PRODUCING
MOSSI WARRIOR CLAN
KOFI PIESIE RESEARCH TEAM

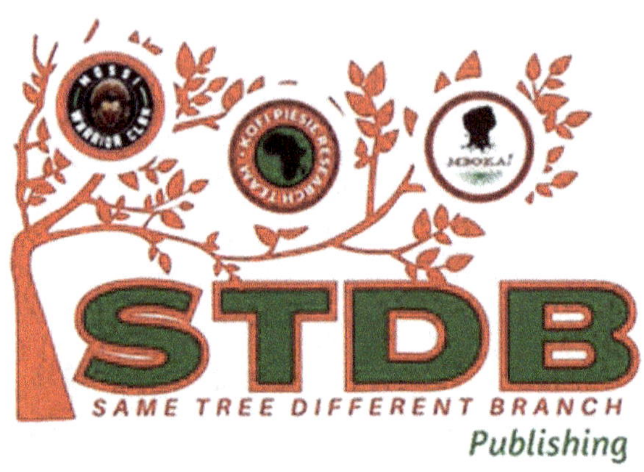

Website:
https://www.sametreedifferentbranchpublishing.com/

Office: 601-695-5797

Email: labarracenelson@yahoo.com

www.ingramcontent.com/pod-product-compliance
Lightning Source LLC
LaVergne TN
LVHW010601110826
845149LV00003B/722

* 9 7 9 8 9 8 9 6 3 7 2 9 4 *